Waking the Tiger
Healing Trauma
The Innate Capacity to Transform
Overwhelming Experiences

Peter A. Levine, Ph.D.

with Ann Frederick

North Atlantic Books
Berkeley, California

Published by
North Atlantic Books
Huichin, unceded Ohlone land
aka Berkeley, California

Cover painting by Guy Coheleach, with permission of the artist
Cover and book design by Andrea DuFlon
Photo by Gerry Greenberg

Printed in the United States of America

Waking the Tiger: Healing Trauma is sponsored and published by North Atlantic Books, an educational nonprofit based in the unceded Ohlone land Huichin (*aka* Berkeley, CA) that collaborates with partners to develop cross-cultural perspectives; nurture holistic views of art, science, the humanities, and healing; and seed personal and global transformation by publishing work on the relationship of body, spirit, and nature.

North Atlantic Books' publications are distributed to the US trade and internationally by Penguin Random House Publisher Services. For further information, visit our website at www.northatlanticbooks.com.

Library of Congress Cataloging–In–Publication Data

Levine, Peter A.
    Waking the tiger; healing trauma/Peter A. Levine.
            p.   cm.
    ISBN-10: 1-55643-233-X
    ISBN-13: 978-1-55643-233-0
    1. Post-traumatic stress disorder—Treatment.   2. Mind and body therapies.   3. Post-traumatic stress disorder—Prevention.
    I. Title
    RC552.P67L48   1997
    616.85'21—dc21   97-3918

24 25 26 27 DATA 25 24 23 22

ogy. Levine effectively argues that the body is healer and that psychological scars of trauma are reversible—but only if we listen to the voices of our body.

Stephen W. Porges, Ph.D.
Professor of Human Development and Psychology,
University of Maryland research scientist studying
the neurophysiological basis of emotional regulation,
stress, and health.

A compelling, almost lyrical trip through the labyrinth of trauma, blending evolutionary insights with pragmatic clinical practice. One cannot help but be drawn into Dr. Levine's theory of traumatization and transformation—a vital contribution to the exciting emerging science of mind/body interaction in the treatment of disease.

Robert C. Scaer, M.D., Neurology
Medical Director, Rehabilitation Services,
Boulder Community Hospital Mapleton Center,
Boulder, CO

Levine knows how to move beyond trauma by engaging the bodily process that should have happened, rather than merely reliving what happened.

Eugene Gendlin, Ph.D.
developer of *Focusing*

Peter Levine has remained at the creative edges of healing, plunging courageously into unknown territories. He has always been consistent—developing an understanding of trauma, its grounding in body tissues, and its healing. This is a book long awaited by students of the healing process.

Don Hanlon Johnson, Ph.D.
Author, Professor of Somatics
California Institute of Integral Studies

Levine's work uncovers the real cause of Traumatic Stress Disorder, thus making it obvious why the usual psychiatric and psychological methods of treating trauma are limited. His approach allows us to "access the problem at its physiological roots through the felt sense. The wisdom of the felt sense gives us at once the instinct of an animal and the intelligence of a human being. Lacking either, we are doomed to repeat our hostilities until none of us remain. With the two working together we can move forward on our evolutionary path and become more truly human—able to use all the capacities that are ours—able to perceive and enjoy our world—able to bring our children into a world that is relatively safe."

Dolores La Chapelle, Director
Way of the Mountain Center
Teacher of Deep Ecology, skiing, and Tai Chi

I find Peter Levine's work very exciting, because he offers the means to deal effectively with the deep trauma frequently present in the cases of hostages, bombing victims, and other victims of terrorism (and their families, who often become victims themselves). In my work with the State Department, and later, as a consultant on terrorist incidents, I learned that one needs a special mix of patience, compassion, and understanding. Clinically sound procedures are needed to identify the layers of traumatizing experience that may be involved, and to help the victims heal by peeling them away. Anyone who must deal with such trauma cases should read this book and seek Peter Levine's help. He does not pretend to present a formula, but he knows and explains the critical pathways.

Terrell E. (Terry) Arnold
Ex-Deputy Director of the Office of Counterterrorism,
US Department of State
Author of *The Violence Formula*

Acknowledgments

To my parents, Morris and Helen, I give thanks for the gift of life, the vehicle for the expression of my work, and for your continued full and unequivocal support from both sides of the physical plane. To Pouncer, the Dingo dog, who has been my guide into the animal world as well a constant companion: at the age of seventeen, you continue to show me the vital joy of corporeal life.

I thank the many ethologists, including Nikolas Tinbergen, Konrad Lorenz, H. von Holst, Paul Leyhausen, and Eibl Elbesfeldt for your naturalistic vision of the human animal, scientific writings, personal correspondence, and encouragement.

I am profoundly indebted to the legacy of Wilhelm Reich, whose monumental contribution to the understanding of energy was taught to me by Philip Curcurruto, a man of simple wisdom and compassionate heart.

To Richard Olney, and Richard Price, who taught me what little I know about self acceptance, and to Ida Rolf for her inspiration and catalysis in forming my identity as a scientist-healer. To Dr. Virginia Johnson, I thank you for your critical understanding of altered states of consciousness.

Theoretical teachers include Ernst Gellhorn, who informed my neuro-physiological thinking, and Akhter Ahsen, who helped consolidate my vision of the "undifferentiated and welded unity of the body and mind."

I thank the many friends, particularly Amy Graybeal and Lorin Hager, who have helped me with the book.

Thanks to Guy Coheleach for kindly allowing me to use his passionate and masterful animal artwork.

Finally, I humbly thank Medusa, Perseus, and the other powerful forces of the body unconscious, for informing my archetypal field of being.

Contents

Traumatic Reaction ▪ Hyperarousal ▪
Constriction ▪ Dissociation/ Exercises ▪
Helplessness ▪ And Then There Was Trauma

If you bring forth that which is within you,
Then that which is within you
Will be your salvation.
If you do not bring forth that which is within you,
Then that which is within you
Will destroy you.
—from the Gnostic Gospels[1]

Introduction

For more than a quarter of a century—half of my life—I have been working to untangle the vast mysteries of trauma. Colleagues and students often ask me how I can possibly remain immersed in a subject as morbid as trauma without completely burning out. The fact is, in spite of having been exposed to bone-chilling anguish and "terrible knowledge," I have become passionately engaged and nourished by this study. It has become my life's work to assist in the understanding and healing of trauma in its many forms. The most common of these forms are automobile and other accidents, serious illness, surgery and other invasive medical and dental procedures, assault, and experiencing or witnessing violence, war, or a myriad of natural disasters.

I am endlessly fascinated with the subject of trauma, with its intricate relationship to the physical and natural sciences, to philosophy, to mythology, and to the arts. Working with trauma has helped me to comprehend the meaning of suffering, both necessary and unnecessary. Most of all, it has helped me to fathom the enigma of the human spirit. I am grateful for this unique opportunity

---

[1]By Elaine Pagels, Random House, 1979

1

to learn, and for the privilege of witnessing and participating in the profound metamorphosis that the healing of trauma can bring about.

Trauma is a fact of life. It does not, however, have to be a life sentence. Not only can trauma be healed, but with appropriate guidance and support, it can be transformative. Trauma has the potential to be one of the most significant forces for psychological, social, and spiritual awakening and evolution. How we handle trauma (as individuals, communities, and societies) greatly influences the quality of our lives. It ultimately affects how or even whether we will survive as a species.

Trauma is traditionally regarded as a psychological and medical disorder of the mind. The practice of modern medicine and psychology, while giving lip service to a connection between mind and body, greatly underestimates the deep relationship that they have in the healing of trauma. The welded unity of body and mind that, throughout time, has formed the philosophical and practical underpinnings of most of the world's traditional healing systems is sadly lacking in our modern understanding and treatment of trauma.

For thousands of years, oriental and shamanic healers have recognized not only that the mind affects the body, as in psychosomatic medicine, but how every organ system of the body equally has a psychic representation in the fabric of the mind. Recent revolutionary developments in neuroscience and psycho-neuro-immunology have established solid evidence of the intricate two-way communication between mind and body. In identifying complex "neuro-peptide messengers," researchers like Candice Pert have discovered many pathways by which mind and body mutually communicate. This leading-edge research echoes what ancient wisdom has always known: that each organ of the body, including the brain, speaks its own "thoughts," "feelings," and "promptings," and listens to those of all the others.

Most trauma therapies address the mind through talk and the molecules of the mind with drugs. Both of these approaches can be of use. However, trauma is not, will not, and can never be fully healed until we also address the essential role played by the body. We must understand how the body is affected by trauma and its central position in healing its aftermath. Without this foundation, our attempts at mastering trauma will be limited and one-sided.

Beyond the mechanistic, reductionistic view of life, there exists a sensing, feeling, knowing, living organism. This living body, a condition we share with all sentient beings, informs us of our innate capacity to heal from the effects of trauma. This book is about the gift of wisdom we receive as a result of learning to harness and transform the body's awesome, primordial, and intelligent energies. In overcoming the destructive force of trauma, our innate potential now lifts us to new heights of mastery and knowledge.

Peter Levine
Written on Amtrak Zephyr
October, 1995

Prologue
Giving the Body Its Due

Body and Mind

> *Whatever increases, decreases, limits or extends the body's power of action, increases decreases, limits, or extends the mind's power of action. And whatever increases, decreases, limits, or extends the mind's power of action, also increases, decreases, limits, or extends the body's power of action.*
> —Spinoza (1632–1677)

If you are experiencing strange symptoms that no one seems to be able to explain, they could be arising from a traumatic reaction to a past event that you may not even remember. You are not alone. You are not crazy. There is a rational explanation for what is happening to you. You have not been irreversibly damaged, and it is possible to diminish or even eliminate your symptoms.

In trauma we know that the mind becomes profoundly altered. For example, a person involved in an auto wreck is protected initially from emotional reaction and even from a clear memory or sense that it really happened. These remarkable mechanisms (e.g., dissociation and

5

denial) allow us to navigate through those critical periods, hopefully waiting for a safe time and place for these altered states to "wear off."

Similarly, the body reacts profoundly in trauma. It tenses in readiness, braces in fear, and freezes and collapses in helpless terror. When the mind's protective reaction to overwhelm returns to normal, the body's response is also meant to normalize after the event. When this restorative process is thwarted, the effects of trauma become fixated and the person becomes traumatized.

Psychology traditionally approaches trauma through its effects on the mind. This is at best only half the story and a wholly inadequate one. Without the body and mind accessed together as a unit, we will not be able to deeply understand or heal trauma.

Finding a Method

This book is about resolving traumatic symptoms using a naturalistic approach I have developed over the past twenty-five years. I do not view post-traumatic stress disorder (PTSD) as pathology to be managed, suppressed, or adjusted to, but the result of a natural process gone awry. Healing trauma requires a direct experience of the living, feeling, knowing organism. The principles I'm going to share with you are the result of working with clients as well as following clues about the origins of trauma. This study has led me into the fields of physiology, neuroscience, animal behavior, mathematics, psychology, and philosophy, to name a few. In the beginning, my successes were the result of happenstance and blind luck. As I continued working with people, questioning what I learned, pushing what I knew further and further into the mystery of trauma, I was able to succeed predictably rather than by chance. Increasingly, I became convinced that the instinctual repertoire of the human organism includes a deep biological knowing which, given the opportunity to do so, can and will guide the process of healing trauma.

While the growing emphasis on attending to these instinctual responses was healing clients, my inquisitiveness was paying off in understanding. People were immensely relieved to finally understand how symptoms were created and to learn how to recognize and experience their own instincts in action.

Somatic Experiencing® is new and is not subject to rigorous scientific research at this time. What I have to support the validity of this approach are several hundred individual cases in which people report that the symptoms which once impaired their ability to live full and satisfied lives are gone or greatly diminished.

I usually work in a one-to-one therapeutic context and often in conjunction with other modalities. Obviously this book cannot replace individual work with a trained therapist. However, I believe that many of the principles and much of the information offered here can be used to facilitate the healing of trauma. If you are in therapy, it may help you to share this book with your therapist. If you are not in therapy, it is possible to use this book to help yourself. However, there are limitations. You may need the guidance of a qualified professional.

The Body As Healer

The body is the shore on the ocean of being.
—Sufi (anonymous)

Section One of this book introduces trauma and explains how post-traumatic symptoms begin, develop, and why they are so compelling and persistent. It lays a foundation of understanding that dispels the tangled web of myths about trauma and replaces them with a simple, coherent description of the basic physiological processes that produce it. While our intellects often override our natural instincts, they do not drive the traumatic reaction. We are more akin to our four-footed friends than we might wish to think.

When I speak of our "organisms," I refer to Webster's definition of "a complex structure of interdependent and subordinate elements whose relations and properties are largely determined by their function in the whole." Organism describes our wholeness, which derives not from the sum of its individual parts, i.e., bones, chemicals, muscles, organs, etc.; it emerges from their dynamic, complex interrelation. Body and mind, primitive instincts, emotions, intellect, and spirituality all need to be considered together in studying the organism. The vehicle through which we experience ourselves as organisms is the "felt sense." The felt sense is a medium through which we experience the fullness of sensation and knowledge about ourselves. You will gain a more clear understanding of these terms as you read through the material and do some of the exercises.

Section One: The Body as Healer—Offers a view of trauma and the process that heals it as natural phenomena. It addresses the innate wisdom to heal that we all have and weaves it into a coherent whole. We'll take a journey into some of our most primitive biological responses. You will emerge from Section One with a fuller appreciation of how your organism operates and how you can work with it to increase your vitality and well-being as well as enhance your overall enjoyment of life, whether or not you have trauma symptoms.

In this section, I refer to exercises that will help you begin to know the felt sense through your own experience. These exercises are important. There is really no other way to convey how this fascinating aspect of the human being operates. Entering the realm of the felt sense is for many people like entering a strange new land, a land they've often visited without ever bothering to notice the scenery. As you read and experience this section, you will find that some of what is said about the way your body works are things that you already know.

Section Two: Symptoms of Trauma—Presents a more in-depth account of the core elements of a traumatic reaction, its symptoms, and the reality a traumatized person lives with.

Section Three: Transformation and Renegotiation—Describes the process by which we can transform our traumas, whether they be personal or societal.

Section Four: First Aid for Trauma—Includes practical information to help prevent trauma from developing after an accident. Also, a brief discussion of childhood trauma. (This latter subject will be covered exclusively in a future book.)

I believe that we all need to understand the essential information in this book. This information deepens our experience and understanding of trauma's healing process and helps us develop a sense reliance on our own organism. Furthermore, I think the information is pertinent on both personal and societal levels. The magnitude of the trauma generated by the events that are affecting our world exact a toll on families, communities, and entire populations. Trauma can be self-perpetuating. Trauma begets trauma and will continue to do so, eventually crossing generations in families, communities and countries until we take steps to contain its propagation. At the moment, the work of transforming trauma within groups of people is still in its infancy. Section Three includes a description of a healing approach used for groups that I am developing with some colleagues in Norway.

Because I often recommend that individuals work- ing therapeutically engage the help of trained profes- sionals as allies in this process, it is my hope that the book will also be of use to these professionals. Few psy- chologists have sufficient background in physiology to recognize the aberrations of experience that can be pro- duced when physiological processes are not allowed to follow a natural course. Ideally, the information in this book will introduce new possibilities for the treatment of trauma. My experience has taught me that many of the currently popular approaches to healing trauma provide only temporary relief at best. Some cathartic methods that encourage intense emotional reliving of trauma may be harmful. I believe that in the long run, cathartic approaches create a dependency on continuing cathar- sis and encourage the emergence of so-called "false memories." Because of the nature of trauma, there is a good chance that the cathartic reliving of an experience can be traumatizing rather than healing.

Psychotherapy deals with a broad spectrum of issues and problems that go far beyond the single topic: shock trauma, the focus of this book. Shock trauma occurs when we experience potentially life-threatening events that overwhelm our capacities to respond effectively. In contrast, people traumatized by ongoing abuse as chil- dren, particularly if the abuse was in the context of their families, may suffer from "developmental trauma." Developmental trauma refers primarily to the psycho- logically based issues that are usually a result of inade- quate nurturing and guidance through critical develop- mental periods during childhood. Although the dynam- ics that produce them are different, cruelty and neglect can result in symptoms that are similar to and often intertwined with those of shock trauma. For this reason, people who have experienced developmental trauma need to enlist the support of a therapist to help them work through the issues that have become intertwined with their traumatic reactions.

When shock trauma is the result of an isolated event or series of events and there is no consistent history of previous trauma, I believe that people, in community with family and friends, have a remarkable ability to bring about their own healing. I strongly encourage this practice. I have written this book in relatively non-technical language. It is also for parents, teachers, child care workers, and others who serve as guides and role models for children to be able to give them a gift of incalculable value by helping them immediately resolve their reactions to traumatic events. In addition, doctors, nurses, paramedics, police, fire fighters, rescue workers, and others who work routinely with the victims of accidents and natural disasters will find this information useful, not only for the work that they do with these traumatized individuals, but for themselves. To witness human carnage of any kind, especially on a regular basis, exacts its own toll and is often as traumatic as experiencing the event firsthand.

How To Use This Book

Give yourself time to absorb the material as you read through the book. Do the exercises suggested in the text. Take it slowly and easily. Trauma is the result of the most powerful drives the human body can produce. It demands respect. You may not hurt yourself by moving through the material quickly or superficially, but you won't get the same benefit that you would if you take the time to digest the information slowly.

If at any time the material or exercises seem disturbing, stop and let things settle. Sit with your experience and see what unfolds. Many of the misconceptions about trauma go surprisingly deep and may affect your experience of as well as your attitude towards yourself. It is important to recognize when this has happened. If you keep a portion of your attention on your reactions to the material, your organism will guide you along at the proper pace.

Body sensation, rather than intense emotion, is the key to healing trauma. Be aware of any emotional reaction swelling up inside you, and be aware of how your body is experiencing these emotions in the form of sensations and thoughts. If your emotions feel too intense, i.e., rage, terror, profound helplessness, etc., you need to enlist competent professional help.

Trauma need not be a life sentence. Of all the maladies that attack the human organism, trauma may ultimately be one that is recognized as beneficial. I say this because in the healing of trauma, a transformation takes place—one that can improve the quality of life. Healing doesn't necessarily require sophisticated drugs, elaborate procedures, or long hours of therapy. When you understand how trauma occurs and when you learn to identify the mechanisms that prevent it from resolving, you will also begin to recognize the ways in which your organism attempts to heal itself. By using a few simple ideas and techniques, you can support rather than impede this innate capacity for healing. The tools presented here will help you move through the trauma and continue on your way with a fuller, more sure sense of yourself. While trauma can be hell on earth, trauma resolved is a gift of the gods—a heroic journey that belongs to each of us.

***No matter where we are, the shadow that trots behind
us is definitely four-footed.***
—Clarissa Pinkola Estes, Ph.D. from Women Who Run
  With The Wolves

I
The Body As Healer

...our mind still has its darkest Africas,
its unmapped Borneos and Amazonian basins.
—Aldous Huxley

1

Shadows From a Forgotten Past

Nature's Plan

A herd of impala grazes peacefully in a lush wadi. Suddenly, the wind shifts, carrying with it a new, but familiar scent. The impala sense danger in the air and become instantly tensed to a hair trigger of alertness. They sniff, look, and listen carefully for a few moments, but when no threat appears, the animals return to their grazing, relaxed yet vigilant.

Seizing the moment, a stalking cheetah leaps from its cover of dense shrubbery. As if it were one organism, the herd springs quickly toward a protective thicket at the wadi's edge. One young impala trips for a split second, then recovers. But it is too late. In a blur, the cheetah lunges toward its intended victim, and the chase is on at a blazing sixty to seventy miles an hour.

At the moment of contact (or just before), the young impala falls to the ground, surrendering to its impending death. Yet, it may be uninjured. The stone-still animal is not pretending to be dead. It has instinctively entered an altered state of consciousness shared by all mammals when death appears imminent. Many indigenous peoples view this phenomenon as a surrender of the spirit of the prey to the predator, which, in a manner of speaking, it is.

Physiologists call this altered state the "immobility" or "freezing" response. It is one of the three primary responses available to reptiles and mammals when faced with an overwhelming threat. The other two, fight and flight, are much more familiar to most of us. Less is known about the immobility response. However, my work over the last twenty-five years has led me to believe that it is the single most important factor in uncovering the mystery of human trauma.

Nature has developed the immobility response for two good reasons. One, it serves as a last-ditch survival strategy. You might know it better as playing possum. Take the young impala, for instance. There is a possibility that the cheetah may decide to drag its 'dead' prey to a place safe from other predators; or to its lair, where the food can be shared later with its cubs. During this time, the impala could awaken from its frozen state and make a hasty escape in an unguarded moment. When it is out of danger, the animal will literally shake off the residual effects of the immobility response and gain full control of its body. It will then return to its normal life as if nothing had happened. Secondly, in freezing, the impala (and human) enters an altered state in which no pain is experienced. What that means for the impala is that it will not have to suffer while being torn apart by the cheetah's sharp teeth and claws.

Most modern cultures tend to judge this instinctive surrender in the face of overwhelming threat as a weakness tantamount to cowardice. However, underneath this judgment lies a deep human fear of immobility. We avoid it because it is a state very similar to death. This avoidance is understandable, but we pay dearly for it. The physiological evidence clearly shows that the ability to go into and come out of this natural response is the key to avoiding the debilitating effects of trauma. It is a gift to us from the wild.

Why Look to the Wild? Trauma is Physiological

> *As surely as we hear the blood in our ears, the echoes of a million midnight shrieks of monkeys, whose last sight of the world was the eyes of a panther, have their traces in our nervous systems.*
> —Paul Shepard[2]

The key to healing traumatic symptoms in humans is in our physiology. When faced with what is perceived as inescapable or overwhelming threat, humans and animals both use the immobility response. The important thing to understand about this function is that it is involuntary. This simply means that the physiological mechanism governing this response resides in the primitive, instinctual parts of our brains and nervous systems, and is not under our conscious control. That is why I feel that the study of wild animal behavior is essential to the understanding and healing of human trauma.

The involuntary and instinctual portions of the human brain and nervous system are virtually identical to those of other mammals and even reptiles. Our brain, often called the triune brain, consists of three integral systems. The three parts are commonly known as the reptilian brain (instinctual), the mammalian or limbic brain (emotional), and the human brain or neo-cortex (rational). Since the parts of the brain that are activated by a perceived life-threatening situation are the parts we share with animals, much can be learned by studying how certain animals, like the impala, avoid traumatiza-

---

[2]The Others—How Animals Made Us Human, Island Press, 1996

tion. To take this one step further, I believe that the key to healing traumatic symptoms in humans lies in our being able to mirror the fluid adaptation of wild animals as they shake out and pass through the immobility response and become fully mobile and functional again.

Unlike wild animals, when threatened we humans have never found it easy to resolve the dilemma of whether to fight or flee. This dilemma stems, at least in part, from the fact that our species has played the role of both predator and prey. Prehistoric peoples, though many were hunters, spent long hours each day huddled together in cold caves with the certain knowledge that they could be snatched up at any moment and torn to shreds.

Our chances for survival increased as we gathered in larger groups, discovered fire, and invented tools, many of which were weapons used for hunting and self-defense. However, the genetic memory of being easy prey has persisted in our brains and nervous systems. Lacking both the swiftness of an impala and the lethal fangs and claws of a stalking cheetah, our human brains often second guess our ability to take life-preserving action. This uncertainty has made us particularly vulnerable to the powerful effects of trauma. Animals like the agile, darting impala know they are prey and are intimate with their survival resources. They sense what they need to do and they do it. Likewise, the sleek cheetah's seventy-miles-an-hour sprint and treacherous fangs and claws make it a self-assured predator.

The line is not so clearly delineated for the human animal. When confronted with a life-threatening situation, our rational brains may become confused and override our instinctive impulses. Though this overriding may be done for a good reason, the confusion that accompanies it sets the stage for what I call the "Medusa

Complex"—the drama called trauma.

As in the Greek myth of Medusa, the human confusion that may ensue when we stare death in the face can turn us to stone. We may literally freeze in fear, which will result in the creation of traumatic symptoms.

Trauma is a pervasive fact of modern life. Most of us have been traumatized, not just soldiers or victims of abuse or attack. Both the sources and consequences of trauma are wide-ranging and often hidden from our awareness. These include natural disasters (e.g., earthquakes, tornadoes, floods, and fires), exposure to violence, accidents, falls, serious illnesses, sudden loss (i.e., a loved one), surgical and other necessary medical and dental procedures, difficult births, and even high levels of stress during gestation.

Fortunately, because we are instinctual beings with the ability to feel, respond, and reflect, we possess the innate potential to heal even the most debilitating traumatic injuries. I am convinced, as well, that we as a global human community can begin to heal from the effects of large-scale social traumas such as war and natural disaster.

It's About Energy

Traumatic symptoms are not caused by the "triggering" event itself. They stem from the frozen residue of energy that has not been resolved and discharged; this residue remains trapped in the nervous system where it can wreak havoc on our bodies and spirits. The long-term, alarming, debilitating, and often bizarre symptoms of PTSD develop when we cannot complete the process of moving in, through and out of the "immobility" or "freezing" state. However, we can thaw by initiating and encouraging our innate drive to return to a state of dynamic equilibrium.

Let's cut to the chase. The energy in our young impala's nervous system as it flees from the pursuing cheetah is charged at seventy miles an hour. The moment the cheetah takes its final lunge, the impala collapses. From the outside, it looks motionless and appears to be dead, but inside, its nervous system is still supercharged at seventy miles an hour. Though it has come to a dead stop, what is now taking place in the impala's body is similar to what occurs in your car if you floor the accelerator and stomp on the brake simultaneously. The difference between the inner racing of the nervous system (engine) and the outer immobility (brake) of the body creates a forceful turbulence inside the body similar to a tornado.

This tornado of energy is the focal point out of which form the symptoms of traumatic stress. To help visualize the power of this energy, imagine that you are making love with your partner, you are on the verge of climax, when suddenly, some outside force stops you. Now, multiply that feeling of withholding by one hundred, and you may come close to the amount of energy aroused by a life-threatening experience.

A threatened human (or impala) must discharge all the energy mobilized to negotiate that threat or it will become a victim of trauma. This residual energy does not simply go away. It persists in the body, and often forces the formation of a wide variety of symptoms e.g., anxiety, depression, and psychosomatic and behavioral problems. These symptoms are the organism's way of containing (or corralling) the undischarged residual energy.

Animals in the wild instinctively discharge all their compressed energy and seldom develop adverse symptoms. We humans are not as adept in this arena. When we are unable to liberate these powerful forces, we become victims of trauma. In our often-unsuccessful attempts to discharge these energies, we may become fixated on them. Like a moth drawn to a flame, we may unknowingly and repeatedly create situations in which the possibility to release ourselves from the trauma trap exists, but without the proper tools and resources most of us fail. The result, sadly, is that many of us become riddled with fear and anxiety and are never fully able to feel at home with ourselves or our world.

Many war veterans and victims of rape know this scenario only too well. They may spend months or even years talking about their experiences, reliving them, expressing their anger, fear, and sorrow, but without passing through the primitive "immobility responses" and releasing the residual energy, they will often remain stuck in the traumatic maze and continue to experience distress.

Fortunately, the same immense energies that create the symptoms of trauma, when properly engaged and mobilized, can transform the trauma and propel us into new heights of healing, mastery, and even wisdom. Trauma resolved is a great gift, returning us to the natural world of ebb and flow, harmony, love, and compassion. Having spent the last twenty-five years working with people who have been traumatized in almost every conceivable fashion, I believe that we humans have the innate capacity to heal not only ourselves, but our world, from the debilitating effects of trauma.

2

The Mystery of Trauma

What is Trauma?

As I was describing my work to a businessman recently, he exclaimed, "Trauma must have been what was wrong with my daughter when she had those screaming fits in her sleep. The psychologist I took her to told me they were 'just nightmares.' I knew they weren't just nightmares." He was right. His daughter had been severely frightened by a routine emergency room procedure and for weeks afterward would scream and cry in her sleep, her body almost completely rigid. The girl's concerned parents were unable to wake her. The odds are very high that she was having a traumatic reaction to her hospital stay.

Many people, like this businessman, have at some point in their lives experienced something inexplicable, or observed something similar in a person close to them. While not all of these unexplained happenings are symptoms of trauma, many are. The "helping" professions tend to describe trauma in terms of the event that caused it, instead of defining it in its own terms. Since we don't

have a way to accurately define trauma, it can be difficult to recognize.

The official definition that psychologists and psychi-
atrists use to diagnose trauma is that it is caused by a
stressful occurrence "that is outside the range of usual
human experience, and that would be markedly distressing to almost anyone."[3] This definition encompasses the following unusual experiences: "serious threat to
one's life or physical integrity; serious threat or harm to
one's children, spouse, or other close relatives or friends;
sudden destruction of one's home or community; seeing
another person who is or has recently been seriously
injured or killed as the result of an accident or physical
violence."

This description is somewhat useful as a starting
point, but it is also vague and misleading. Who can say
what is "outside the range of usual human experience",
or "markedly distressing to almost anyone"? The events
mentioned in the definition are helpful qualifiers, but
there are many other potentially traumatizing events
that fall into gray areas. Accidents, falls, illnesses, and
surgeries that the body unconsciously perceives as
threatening are often not consciously regarded as outside
the range of usual human experience. However, they are
often traumatizing. In addition, rapes, drive-by shootings, and other tragedies occur frequently in many communities. Though they may be considered inside the
range of usual experience, rapes and shootings will
always be traumatic.

The healing of trauma depends upon the recognition of its symptoms. Because traumatic symptoms are
largely the result of primitive responses, they are often
difficult to recognize. People don't need a definition of
trauma; we need an experiential sense of how it feels. A

[3]Diagnostic Statistics Manual—DSM III, Revised Edition, 1993

client of mine described the following experience:

> My five-year-old son and I were playing ball in the park
> when he threw the ball a long distance away from me.
> While I was retrieving the ball, he ran into a busy street
> to get another ball he had spotted. As I reached to pick
> up the ball we had been playing with, I heard the tires of
> a car screech long and loud. I knew instantly that Joey
> had been hit by the car. My heart seemed to fall into the
> pit of my stomach. All the blood in my body seemed to
> stop circulating and fell down to my feet. Feeling pale as
> a ghost, I started running toward the crowd gathering
> in the street. My legs were as heavy as lead. Joey was
> nowhere in sight, yet with the certainty that he had been
> involved in the accident, my heart tightened and con-
> stricted, then expanded to fill my chest with dread. I
> pushed through the crowd and collapsed on top of Joey's
> still body. The car had dragged his body several feet
> before it stopped. His body was scratched and bloody, his
> clothes were torn, and he was so still. Feeling panic-strick-
> en and helpless, I frantically tried to piece him
> back together. I tried to wipe away the blood, but only
> succeeded in spreading it. I tried to pat his torn clothes
> back into place. I kept thinking, "No, this isn't happen-
> ing. Breathe, Joey, breathe." As though my life force
> could infuse life into his still body, I kept collapsing on
> top of him, pressing my heart against his. A numbness
> began to creep over me as I felt myself pulling away from
> the scene. I was just going through the motions now. I
> couldn't feel anymore.

People who have experienced trauma of this magnitude
really know what it is, and their responses to it are basic
and primitive. With this unfortunate woman the symptoms were brutally clear and compelling. For many of us,
however, the symptoms are more subtle. We can learn to

identify a traumatic experience by exploring our own reactions. It has a feel that is unmistakable once it is identified. Lets look at an event that is clearly outside the range of ordinary experience.

Chowchilla, California

On a sweltering summer day in 1976, twenty-six children ranging in age from five to fifteen years were kidnapped from their school bus outside a small California town. They were shoved into two dark vans, driven to an abandoned quarry, and then imprisoned in an underground vault for approximately thirty hours. They escaped, and were immediately taken to a local hospital. There, they received treatment for physical injuries, but were returned home without even cursory psychological examinations. As far as the two hospital physicians could tell, the children were "all right." The doctors simply did not recognize that anything was wrong or that the children's progress would need to be closely monitored. A few days later a local psychiatrist was asked to address the Chowchilla parents. He stated emphatically that there might be a psychological problem in only one of the twenty-six children. He was expressing the standard psychiatric belief at that time.

Eight months after the event, another psychiatrist, Lenore Terr, began one of the first scientific follow-up studies of children who had been traumatized. The study included these children. Rather than one in the twenty-six children showing aftereffects, Terr found the reverse to be true—nearly all of the children showed severe long-term effects on their psychological, medical, and social functioning. For many of these children the nightmare had just begun. They experienced recurring nightmares, violent tendencies, and impaired ability to function normally in personal and social relations. The effects were so debilitating that the lives and family structures of these children were all but destroyed in the years that followed. The one child who was less severely affected was fourteen-year-old Bob Barklay. Here is a brief summary of what happened to him during the traumatic event.

The children had been imprisoned in "the hole" (a trailer buried beneath hundreds of pounds of dirt and rock in an abandoned quarry) for nearly a day when one of them leaned against a wooden pole that was supporting the roof. The makeshift support fell and the ceiling began to collapse on them. By this time, most of them were suffering from severe shock—frozen and apathetic, they were almost unable to move. Those who realized the seriousness of the situation began to scream. These children could see that if they weren't able to escape soon, they would all die. It was in this moment of crisis that Bob Barklay enlisted the help of another boy to dig their way out. Following Bob's lead, the boys were able to scoop out enough dirt to dig a small tunnel through the ceiling and into the quarry.

Bob was able to respond to the crisis and remain actively mobilized throughout the escape. Even though the other children escaped with him, many of them seemed to experience more fear in escaping their entombment. If they had not been urged strongly to flee, they would have remained there—helpless. Moving like zombies, they had to be ushered out to freedom. This passivity is similar to the behavior noted by military teams that specialize in the freeing of hostages. It is called the "Stockholm syndrome." Often, hostages will not move unless repeatedly commanded to do so.

The Mystery of Trauma

By bringing the other children to freedom, Bob Barklay successfully met an extraordinary challenge. On that day at Chowchilla he was unquestionably a hero. However, what is more significant for his life, and for anyone interested in trauma, is that he emerged without the same degree of debilitating traumatic aftereffects as did the other twenty-five children. He was able to stay in motion and flow through the immobility response that completely overwhelmed and incapacitated the others. Some were so frightened that their fear continued to overwhelm and immobilize them long after the actual danger had passed.

This is a theme present in traumatized people. They are unable to overcome the anxiety of their experience. They remain overwhelmed by the event, defeated and terrified. Virtually imprisoned by their fear, they are unable to re-engage in life. Others who experience similar events may have no enduring symptoms at all. Trauma affects some of us in mysterious ways. This is one of them. No matter how frightening an event may seem, not everyone who experiences it will be traumatized. Why do some people, like Bob Barklay, successfully meet such challenges while others, who seem no less intelligent or capable, become completely debilitated? Of greater import, what are the implications concerning those of us who are already debilitated from prior traumas?

Waking the Tiger: A First Glimmering

Trauma was a complete mystery to me when I first began working with it. My first major breakthrough in understanding came quite unexpectedly in 1969 when I was asked to see a woman, Nancy, who was suffering from intense panic attacks. The attacks were so severe that she was unable to leave her house alone. She was referred to me by a psychiatrist who knew of my interest in body/mind approaches to healing (a fledgling and obscure field at that time). He thought that some kind of relaxation training might be helpful.

Relaxation was not the answer. In our first session, as I naively, and with the best of intentions, attempted to help her relax, she went into a full-blown anxiety attack. She appeared paralyzed and unable to breathe. Her heart was pounding wildly, and then seemed to almost stop. I became quite frightened. Had I paved the yellow brick road to hell? We entered together into her nightmarish attack.

Surrendering to my own intense fear, yet somehow managing to remain present, I had a fleeting vision of a tiger jumping toward us. Swept along with the experience, I exclaimed loudly, "You are being attacked by a large tiger. See the tiger as it comes at you. Run toward that tree; climb it and escape!" To my surprise, her legs started trembling in running movements. She let out a bloodcurdling scream that brought in a passing police officer (fortunately my office partner somehow managed to explain the situation). She began to tremble, shake, and sob in full-bodied convulsive waves.

Nancy continued to shake for almost an hour. She recalled a terrifying memory from her childhood. When she was three years old she had been strapped to a table for a tonsillectomy. The anesthesia was ether. Unable to move, feeling suffocated (common reactions to ether), she had terrifying hallucinations. This early experience had a deep impact on her. Like the traumatized children at Chowchilla, Nancy was threatened, overwhelmed, and as a result, had become physiologically stuck in the immobility response. In other words, her body had literally resigned itself to a state where the act of escaping could not exist. Along with this resignation came the pervasive loss of her real and vital self as well as loss of a secure and spontaneous personality. Twenty years after the traumatizing event, the subtle and hidden effects emerged. Nancy was in a crowded room taking the Graduate Records Examination when she went into a severe panic attack. Later, she developed agoraphobia (fear of leaving her house alone). The experience was so extreme and seemingly irrational that she knew she must seek help.

After the breakthrough that came in our initial visit, Nancy left my office feeling, in her words, "like she had herself again." Although we continued working together for a few more sessions, where she gently trembled and shook, the anxiety attack she experienced that day was her last. She stopped taking medication to control her attacks and subsequently entered graduate school, where she completed her doctorate without relapse.

At the time I met Nancy, I was studying animal predator-prey behaviors. I was intrigued by the similarity between Nancys paralysis when her panic attack began and what happened to the impala described in the last chapter. Most prey animals use immobility when attacked by a larger predator from which they can't escape. I am quite certain that these studies strongly influenced the fortuitous vision of the imaginary tiger. For several years after that I worked to understand the significance of Nancy's anxiety attack and her response to the image of the tiger. There were many detours and wrong turns along the way.

I now know that it was not the dramatic emotional catharsis and reliving of her childhood tonsillectomy that was catalytic in her recovery, but the discharge of energy she expe-

rienced when she flowed out of her passive, frozen immobility response into an active, successful escape. The image of the tiger awoke her instinctual, responsive self. The other profound insight that I gleaned from Nancy's experience was that the resources that enable a person to succeed in the face of a threat can be used for healing. This is true not just at the time of the experience, but even years after the event.

I learned that it was unnecessary to dredge up old memories and relive their emotional pain to heal trauma. In fact, severe emotional pain can be re-traumatizing. What we need to do to be freed from our symptoms and fears is to arouse our deep physiological resources and consciously utilize them. If we remain ignorant of our power to change the course of our instinctual responses in a proactive rather than reactive way, we will continue being imprisoned and in pain.

Bob Barklay minimized the traumatic impact of his experience by remaining engaged in the task of freeing himself and the other children from the underground vault. The focused energy he expended in doing so is the key to why he was less traumatized than the other children. He not only became a hero in the moment, but he also helped free his nervous system from being overburdened by undischarged energy and fear for years to come.

Nancy became a heroine twenty years after her ordeal. The running movements made by her legs when she responded to the make-believe tiger allowed her to do the same thing. This response helped rid her nervous system of the excess energy that had been mobilized to deal with the threat she experienced during her tonsillectomy. She was able, long after the original trauma, to awaken her capacity for heroism and actively escape— as Bob Barklay did. The long-term results for Bob and

Nancy were similar. Released from the debilitating effects that plague so many trauma sufferers, they were both able to move on with their lives. As the work developed I learned that the healing process was more effective if it was less dramatic, occurring more gradually. The most important lesson I have gleaned is that we all have the innate capacity to heal our traumas.

When we are unable to flow through trauma and complete instinctive responses, these incompleted actions often undermine our lives. Unresolved trauma can keep us excessively cautious and inhibited, or lead us around in ever-tightening circles of dangerous re-enactment, victimization, and unwise exposure to danger. We become the perpetual victims or therapy clients. Trauma can destroy the quality of our relationships and distort sexual experiences. Compulsive, perverse, promiscuous, and inhibited sexual behaviors are common symptoms of trauma—not just sexual trauma. The effects of trauma can be pervasive and global or they can be subtle and elusive. When we do not resolve our traumas, we feel that we have failed, or that we have been betrayed by those we chose to help us. We need not blame this failure and betrayal on ourselves or others. The solution to the problem lies in increasing our knowledge about how to heal trauma.

Until we understand that traumatic symptoms are physiological as well as psychological, we will be woefully inadequate in our attempts to heal them. The heart of the matter lies in being able to recognize that trauma represents animal instincts gone awry. When harnessed, these instincts can be used by the conscious mind to transform traumatic symptoms into a state of well-being.

Acts must be carried through to their completion.
Whatever their point of departure, the end will be
beautiful. It is (only) because an action has not been
completed that it is vile.
—Jean Genet, from Thiefs Journal

3

Wounds That Can Heal

When a young tree is injured it grows around that injury. As the tree continues to develop, the wound becomes relatively small in proportion to the size of the tree. Gnarly burls and misshapen limbs speak of injuries and obstacles encountered through time and overcome. The way a tree grows around its past contributes to its exquisite individuality, character, and beauty. I certainly don't advocate traumatization to build character, but since trauma is almost a given at some point in our lives, the image of the tree can be a valuable mirror.

Although human beings have been experiencing trauma for thousands of years, it is only in the last ten years that it has begun to receive widespread professional and public attention. Trauma is now a household word, with true confessions from stars appearing in weekly supermarket tabloids. In that context, trauma has been associated primarily with sexual abuse. In spite of growing professional interest, and the sensationalism and saturation of the media, we see little evidence of trauma being healed.

Statistics show that as many as one in three women and one in five men have been sexually abused as children. Even with the increased recognition of sexual abuse, there remains little understanding about the conditions necessary for its healing. For example, many traumatized individuals identify and cluster together as victims. While this can be a useful first step to healing, it can interfere with recovery if continued indefinitely. Sexual abuse is one of many forms of trauma. No matter what the source may be, we are much more likely to heal from the effects of trauma by creating a positive framework. The image of the mature tree, full of character and beauty, will serve us better than denying the experience or identifying ourselves as victims and survivors.

The roots of trauma lie in our instinctual physiologies. As a result, it is through our bodies, as well as our minds, that we discover the key to its healing. Each of us must find those roots, realizing that we have a choice—perhaps one of the greatest in our lives. The healing of trauma is a natural process that can be accessed through an inner awareness of the body. It does not require years of psychological therapy, or that memories be repeatedly dredged up and expunged from the unconscious. We will see that the endless search for and retrieval of so-called "traumatic memories" can often interfere with the organisms innate wisdom to heal.

My observations of scores of traumatized people has led me to conclude that post-traumatic symptoms are, fundamentally, incomplete physiological responses suspended in fear. Reactions to life-threatening situations remain symptomatic until they are completed. Post-traumatic stress is one example. These symptoms will not go away until the responses are discharged and completed. Energy held in immobility can be transformed, as we have seen in the cases of Bob Barklay and Nancy (see Chapter Two). Both of these people succeeded in a biological mobilization and discharge of survival energy that allowed them to return to full vitality.

A bird that crashes into a window, mistaking it for open sky, will appear stunned or even dead. A child who sees the bird's collision with the glass may have a hard time keeping away from the wounded animal. The child may pick the bird up out of curiosity, concern, or a desire to help. The warmth of the child's hands can facilitate the bird's return to normal functioning. As the bird begins to tremble, it will show signs that it is reorienting to its surroundings. It may stagger slightly, try to regain its balance, and look around. If the bird is not injured and is allowed to go through the trembling-reorienting process without interruption, it can move through its immobilization and fly away without being traumatized. If the trembling is interrupted, the animal may suffer serious consequences. If the child tries to pet the animal when it begins to show signs of life, the reorienting process may be disrupted, propelling the bird back into shock. If the discharge process is repeatedly disturbed, each successive state of shock will last longer. As a result, the bird may die of fright—overwhelmed by its own helplessness.

Although we rarely die, humans suffer when we are unable to discharge the energy that is locked in by the freezing response. The traumatized veteran, the rape survivor, the abused child, the impala, and the bird all have been confronted by overwhelming situations. If they are unable to orient and choose between fight or flight, they will freeze or collapse. Those who are able to discharge that energy will be restored. Rather than moving through the freezing response, as animals do routinely, humans often begin a downward spiral characterized by an increasingly debilitating constellation of symptoms. To move through trauma we need quietness, safety, and protection similar to that offered the bird in the gentle warmth of the child's hands. We need support from friends and relatives, as well as from nature. With this support and connection, we can begin to trust and honor the natural process that will bring us to completion and wholeness, and eventually peace.

Oliver Sacks, the author of *Awakenings, The Man Who Mistook His Wife for a Hat,* and *Migraine,* describes in the third of these books the compelling attacks of several patients. Migraines are a nervous system stress reaction that is quite similar and often related to post-traumatic (freezing) reactions. Sacks gives a fascinating account of a mathematician with a weekly migraine cycle. On Wednesday the mathematician would get nervous and irritable. By Thursday or Friday the stress would worsen so much that he was unable to work. On Saturday he would become greatly agitated, and on Sunday he would have a full-blown migraine attack. By that afternoon, however, the migraine dissipated and died away. In the wake of the migraine discharge, the man experienced a creative, hopeful rebirth. On Monday and Tuesday he would feel refreshed, rejuvenated, and renewed. Calm and creative, he would work effectively until Wednesday, when the irritability started again and the whole cycle would repeat.

By using medication to alleviate this patient's migraine symptoms, Sacks realized that he had also blocked the man's creative source. Dr. Sacks laments, "When I 'cured' this man of his migraines, I also 'cured' him of his mathematics… Along with the pathology, the creativity also disappeared." Sacks explains that patients may break into a gentle sweat and pass pints of urine in what he describes as "a physiological catharsis" after migraine attacks. Such reactions did not occur when the man was medicated. Similarly, gentle beads of warm sweat often accompany the resolution and healing of trauma. In moving through apprehensive chills to mounting excitement and waves of moist tingling warmth, the body, with its innate capacity to heal, melts the iceberg created by deeply frozen trauma. Anxiety and despair can become a creative wellspring when we allow ourselves to experience bodily sensations, such as trembling, that stem from traumatic symptoms.

Held within the symptoms of trauma are the very energies, potentials, and resources necessary for their constructive transformation. The creative healing process can be blocked in a number of ways—by using drugs to suppress symptoms, by overemphasizing adjustment or control, or by denial or invalidation of feelings and sensations.

Trauma Is Not a Disease But a Dis-Ease

In his 1992 *New York Times* article, "Wounds That Can Not Heal," Daniel Golman, a leading popular science writer, reports on the prevalent medical view that trauma is an irreversible disease. Hope is held that a magic bullet (like Prozac) will be found to cure this "brain disease." Golman quotes Dr. Dennis Charney, a Yale psychiatrist:

> It does not matter if it was the incessant terror of combat, trapped in a hurricane...or an auto accident...all uncontrollable stress can have the same biological impact...Victims of a devastating trauma *may never be the same biologically.* [emphasis added]."

Trauma evokes a biological response that needs to remain fluid and adaptive, not stuck and maladaptive. A maladaptive response is not necessarily a disease, but a dis-ease—a discomfort that can range from mild uneasiness to downright debilitation. The potential for fluidity still exists in maladaption and must be tapped for the restoration of ease and full functioning. If these trapped energies are not allowed to move, and trauma becomes chronic, it can take a great deal of time and/or energy to restore the person to equilibrium and health.

In the same *New York Times* article, Golman quotes Dr. Nemeroff, another researcher:

> If a car backfires at the mall parking lot, it floods you with the same feelings as the original trauma; you start sweating, you're scared, you have chills and the shakes...

The next step this researcher suggests is "to develop drugs that counter this [shaking] reaction." Drugs may be useful in buying time to help the traumatized individual stabilize. However, when they are used for prolonged periods to suppress the body's own balancing response to stress, they interfere with healing. To complete its biological and meaningful course of action, the organism requires the spontaneous shaking and trembling that we see throughout the animal world. In a 1982 National Geographic video entitled "Polar Bear Alert," this phenomenon can be viewed clearly. A polar bear, after a stressful chase, is shot with a tranquilizer dart. As it slowly wakens from the anesthesia, the bear goes through an extended period of shaking and trembling before returning to normal.

In viewing trauma as a disease, medicine too often seeks to suppress this natural and creative process, as it did with Dr. Sacks' migraine patient. Whether the restorative response is suppressed by drugs, held in frozen fear, or controlled by sheer acts of will, the innate capacity for self-regulation becomes derailed.

Contrary to popular belief, trauma can be healed. Not only can it be healed, but in many cases it can be healed without long hours of therapy; without the painful reliving of memories; and without a continuing reliance on medication. We must realize that it is neither necessary nor possible to change past events. Old trauma symptoms are examples of bound-up energy and lost lessons. The past doesn't matter when we learn how to be present; every moment becomes new and creative. We have only to heal our present symptoms and proceed. A healing moment ripples forward and back, out and about.

Trauma can be prevented more easily than it can be healed. With the information and tools described in this book, the effects of potential traumatic experiences can be prevented and an individual's resiliency to later threatening situations can be enhanced. In many cases, the tools and ideas presented here will help transform the symptoms of even long-standing traumas into life-affirming experiences. These techniques can be used with at-risk children, a spouse, or friends to create a positive support network. Of course, it must also be realized that some people have been traumatized to the degree that they may require professional help, including appropriate medication, to assist them in their recovery. There is no shame or inadequacy in seeking that support. You may wish to share this material with your therapist or doctor so that he or she can best work with you.

4

A Strange New Land

Trauma Is Not a Life Sentence

Some of the frightening and often bizarre symptoms suffered by traumatized people include: flashbacks, anxiety, panic attacks, insomnia, depression, psychosomatic complaints, lack of openness, violent unprovoked rage attacks, and repetitive destructive behaviors. People who were once healthy can be propelled to the "edge of insanity" as the result of events that occur within a relatively short period of time. Bring up the subject of trauma and most people think of war veterans, or people who were severely abused as children.

Trauma has become so commonplace that most people don't even recognize its presence. It affects everyone. Each of us has had a traumatic experience at some time in our lives, regardless of whether it left us with an obvious case of post-traumatic stress. Because trauma symptoms can remain hidden for years after a triggering event, some of us who have been traumatized are not yet symptomatic.

Both the causes and the symptoms of trauma are

incredibly vast and diverse. Today, it is understood that trauma is a common occurrence that can be caused by seemingly benign events. The good news is that we don't have to live with it—at least, not forever. Trauma can be healed, and even more easily prevented. Its most bizarre symptoms can be resolved if we are willing to let our natural, biological instincts guide us. To accomplish this, we need to learn a whole new way of understanding and experiencing ourselves. For most of us its going to be like living in a strange new land.

The Strange New Land

I'm going to take you into the dark, primeval regions of the world that were once inhabited solely by reptiles. This primitive world is still very much alive in us. It is still home to some of our most valuable personal resources. Most of us are taught to ignore these innate resources and depend upon the "advantages" offered by technology. We choose to accept this solution without realizing that we have given up important parts of ourselves. Perhaps we are unaware that we have made this choice.

When humans roamed the hills and valleys, gathered roots and berries, hunted wild animals, and lived in caves, our existence was closely linked to the natural world. Every day, every minute, and every second we were prepared to defend ourselves, our families, and allies from predators and other dangers—often at the risk of our own lives. The irony is that the life-threatening events prehistoric people routinely faced molded our modern nervous systems to respond powerfully and fully whenever we perceive our survival to be threatened. To this day, when we exercise this natural capacity, we feel exhilarated and alive, powerful, expanded, full of energy, and ready to take on any challenge. Being threatened engages our deepest resources and allows us to experience our fullest potential as human beings. In turn, our emotional and physical well-being is enhanced.

Modern life offers us few overt opportunities to use this powerfully evolved capacity. Today, our survival depends increasingly on developing our ability to think rather than being able to physically respond. Consequently, most of us have become separated from our natural, instinctual selves—in particular, the part of us that can proudly, not disparagingly, be called animal. Regardless of how we view ourselves, in the most basic sense we literally are human animals. The fundamental challenges we face today have come about relatively quickly, but our nervous systems have been much slower to change. It is no coincidence that people who are more in touch with their natural selves tend to fare better when it comes to trauma. Without easy access to the resources of this primitive, instinctual self, humans alienate their bodies from their souls. Most of us don't think of or experience ourselves as animals. Yet, by not living through our instincts and natural reactions, we aren't fully human either. Existing in a limbo in which we are neither animal nor fully human can cause a number of problems, one of which is being susceptible to trauma.

In order to stay healthy, our nervous systems and psyches need to face challenges and to succeed in meeting those challenges. When this need is not met, or when we are challenged and cannot triumph, we end up lacking vitality and are unable to fully engage in life. Those of us who have been defeated by war, abuse, accidents, and other traumatic events suffer far more severe consequences.

Trauma!

Few people question the seriousness of the problems created by trauma, yet we have difficulty comprehending how many people are affected by it. In a recent study of more than one thousand men and women, it was found that forty percent had gone through a traumatic event in the past three years. Most often cited were: being raped or physically assaulted; being in a serious accident; witnessing someone else being killed or injured. As many as thirty percent of the homeless people in this country are thought to be Vietnam veterans suffering from post-traumatic stress. Somewhere between seventy-five and one hundred million Americans have experienced childhood sexual and physical abuse. The conservative AMA estimates that over thirty percent of all married women, as well as thirty percent of pregnant women, have been beaten by their spouses. One woman is beaten by her husband or lover every nine seconds (the beatings of pregnant women are also traumatic to the fetus).

War and violence have affected the lives of nearly every man, woman, and child living on this planet. In the last few years, entire communities have been wiped out or devastated by natural disasters—Hurricane Hugo, Andrew, and Iniki; flooding of the Midwest and California; the Oakland Fire; the Loma Prieta, Los Angeles, Mexico City, Cairo, and Kobe Earthquakes; and many more. All of the people affected by these events are at risk or are already suffering from trauma.

Many other people have traumatic symptoms that go unrecognized. For example, ten to fifteen percent of all adults suffer from panic attacks, unexplained anxiety, or phobias. As many as seventy-five percent of the people who go to doctors have complaints that are labeled psychosomatic because no physical explanation can be found for them. My work leads me to believe that many of these people have traumatic histories which at least contribute to their symptoms. Depression and anxiety often have traumatic antecedents, as does mental illness. A study conducted by Bessel van der Kolk[4], a respected researcher in the field of trauma, has shown that patients at a large mental institution frequently had symptoms indicative of trauma. Many of these symptoms were overlooked at the time because no one recognized their significance.

Today, most people are aware of the fact that sexual, physical, and emotional abuse, as well as exposure to violence or danger, can profoundly alter a person's life. What most people don't know is that many seemingly benign situations can be traumatic. The consequences of trauma can be widespread and hidden. Over the course of my career I have found an extraordinary range of symptoms—behavioral and psychosomatic problems, lack of vitality, etc.—related not only to the traumatic events mentioned above, but also to quite ordinary events.

Common occurrences can produce traumatic after-effects that are just as debilitating as those experienced by veterans of combat or survivors of childhood abuse. Traumatic effects are not always apparent immediately following the incidents that caused them. Symptoms can remain dormant, accumulating over years or even decades. Then, during a stressful period, or as the result of another incident, they can show up without warning. There may also be no indication of the original cause. Thus, a seemingly minor event can give rise to a sudden breakdown, similar to one that might be caused by a single catastrophic event.

[4]Psychological Trauma—American Psychiatric Press, 1987

What We Don't Know Can Hurt Us

When it comes to trauma, what we don't know can hurt us. Not knowing we are traumatized doesn't prevent us from having problems that are caused by it. However, with the incredible maze of misinformation and myth that exists about trauma and its treatment, the denial is understandable.

It is difficult enough to deal solely with the symptoms of trauma without the added anxiety of not knowing why we are experiencing them or whether they will ever cease. Anxiety can crop up for a variety of reasons, including a deep pain that comes when your spouse, friends, and relatives unite in the conviction that its time for you to get on with your life. They want you to act normally because they believe you should have learned to live with your symptoms by now. There are feelings of hopelessness, futility, and despair that accompany being incorrectly advised that the only way your symptoms can be alleviated is through a lifelong regime of medication or therapy. Estrangement and fear can arise from the thought of talking to anyone about your symptoms, because your symptoms are so bizarre you are certain that no one else could be experiencing the same thing. You also suspect that no one will believe you if you do tell them, and that you are probably going crazy. There is the added stress associated with mounting medical bills as you go in for a third or fourth round of tests, procedures, referrals, and finally, exploratory surgery to ascertain the cause of your mysterious pain. You live with the knowledge that the doctors believe you are a hypochondriac because no cause for your condition can be found.

When interpreting trauma symptoms, jumping to the wrong conclusions can also be devastating. Harmful consequences can ensue when inaccurate readings of symptoms lead people to believe they were sexually, physically, or even ritually abused as children, when they were not. I am in no way suggesting that childhood abuse does not occur. Large numbers of children in every segment of society suffer unconscionable abuses every day. Many of them do not remember the abuses until they become adults. However, as I will explain in later chapters, the dynamics of trauma are such that they can produce frightening and bizarre "memories" of past events that seem extremely real, but never happened.

The body of misinformation about trauma, its treatment, and a traumatized person's prospects for recovery is astounding. Even many professionals who specialize in trauma don't understand it. Inevitably, misinformation leads to anxiety and more suffering.

A Traumatized Persons Reality

All of us have had experiences that lose something in the telling. Shrugging it off, we say, "You had to be there." Trauma is such an experience. Words can't accurately convey the anguish that a traumatized person experiences. It has an intensity that defies description. Many traumatized people feel that they live in a personal hell in which no other human could possibly share. While this is not entirely true, elements of this perception are accurate. Here is a condensation of what severely traumatized individuals struggle with: *I don't know of one thing I don't fear. I fear getting out of bed in the morning. I fear walking out of my house. I have great fears of death...not that I will die someday, but that I am going to die within the next few minutes. I fear anger...my own and everyone else's, even when anger is not present. I fear rejection and/or abandonment. I fear success and failure. I get pain in my chest, and tingling and numbness in my arms and legs every day. I almost daily experience cramps ranging from menstrual-type cramps to intense pain. I just really hurt most of the time. I feel that I can't go on. I have headaches. I feel nervous all the time. I have shortness of breath, racing heart, disorientation, and panic. I'm always cold, and I have dry mouth. I have trouble swallowing. I have no energy or motivation, and when I do accomplish something, I feel no sense of satisfaction. I feel overwhelmed, confused, lost, helpless, and hopeless daily. I have uncontrollable outbursts of rage and depression.*

Get On with Your Life

If it hurts, hide it.
—Michael Martin Murphy from Cowboy Logic

Because the symptoms and emotions associated with trauma can be extreme, most of us (and those close to us) will recoil and attempt to repress these intense reactions. Unfortunately, this mutual denial can prevent us from healing. In our culture there is a lack of tolerance for the emotional vulnerability that traumatized people experience. Little time is allotted for the working through of emotional events. We are routinely pressured into adjusting too quickly in the aftermath of an overwhelming situation.

Denial is so common in our culture that it has become a cliché. How often have you heard these words? "Pull yourself together, its over now. You should forget about it. Grin and bear it. It's time to get on with your life."

Who Is Traumatized?

Our ability to respond appropriately when faced with danger and threat is determined by a number of different factors:

The event itself. How threatening is it? How long does it last? How often does it occur? Threatening events that are intense and continuous present the greatest challenges. Severely threatening incidents that occur repeatedly (but with some reprieve) can be equally challenging. War and childhood abuse are two of the most common examples of traumatizing events that often exceed an individual's survival resources.

The context of a persons life at the time of the traumatizing event. Support (or lack of it) by family and friends can have a dramatic impact on us. Also significant is the toll taken by poor health, ongoing stress, fatigue, or poor nutrition.

Physical characteristics of the individual. Some people are constitutionally (genetically) more resilient to stressful events than others. Strength, speed, and overall physical fitness can also be important in some situations. Even more important is a person's age or level of physiological development and resilience. Being left alone in a cold room can be totally overwhelming to an infant, frightening to a toddler, distressing to a ten-year-old, and only mildly uncomfortable to an adolescent or adult.

A person's learned capabilities. Infants and children, or anyone lacking the experience or skills to handle a threatening situation, are more vulnerable to traumatization. In the example above, an adolescent or an adult cannot only tolerate the cold and isolation more easily, they can also complain, look for a thermostat, try to leave the room, put on a sweater, or just rub their arms. In varying degrees these options are not available to a younger child or infant. Because of this fact, traumatic reactions often track back to early childhood. It is important to remember that a traumatic reaction is valid regardless of how the event that induced it appears to anyone else.

The individual's experienced sense of his or her capacity to meet danger. Some people experience themselves as completely capable of defending themselves against danger while others don't. This experienced sense of self-confidence is significant, and is not completely determined by our available resources for dealing with threatening situations. These resources can be either internal or external.

External resources. What the environment provides in the way of potential safety (e.g., a tall sturdy tree, rocks, a narrow crevice, a good hiding place, a weapon, a helpful friend) contributes to our inner sense of resourcefulness, if our developmental level is such that we can take advantage of it. For a child, an external resource could be an adult who meets the child with respect rather than abuse, or it could be a place of safety where abuse does not occur. A resource (especially for children) can come in many forms—an animal, a tree, a stuffed toy, or even an angel.

Internal resources. Internally, a person's experienced sense of self is affected by a complex array of resources. These resources include psychological attitudes and experience, but even more important are the instinctual responses known as innate action plans that are deeply embedded in the organism. All animals, including humans, use these instinctive solutions to improve their chances of survival. They are like the preset programs that govern all of our basic biological responses (e.g., eating, resting, reproducing, and defending). In a healthy person, the nervous system brings these innate defense action plans to the fore whenever a threat is perceived. For example: your arm suddenly raises to protect you from a (consciously) unnoticed ball thrown in your direction; or, when you duck a fraction of a second before you walk into a low-hanging branch. Innate action plans also involve the fight and flight reactions.

In a more complex example, I was told the following story by a woman: she is walking home in the dark when she sees two men coming toward her on the opposite side of the street. Something about their demeanor doesn't feel right, and the woman becomes immediately alert. As they come closer, the two men split up, one angles toward her across the street, the other circles around behind her. What was suspicion before is now confirmed—she is in danger. Her heart rate increases, she feels suddenly more alert, and her mind searches wildly for an optimal response. Should she scream? Should she run? Where should she run to? What should she scream? Choices tumble through her mind at a frenetic rate. She has too many options to choose from and not enough time to consider them. Dramatically, instinct takes over. Without consciously deciding what to do, she suddenly finds herself moving with firm, quick steps straight toward the man angling across the street. Visibly startled by her boldness, the man veers off in another direction. The man behind her melts into the shadows as the man in front of her loses his strategic position. They are confused. She is safe.

Thanks to her ability to trust her instinctual flow, this woman was not traumatized. Despite her initial confusion about what to do, she followed one of her innate defense action plans and successfully avoided the attack.

A similar behavior was reported of Misha, a two-year-old Siberian Husky described in Elizabeth Thomas' delightful book, *The Hidden Life of Dogs*. On one of his evening jaunts, Misha encountered a large, fierce Saint Bernard and was trapped between it and the highway: "...for a few seconds things looked bad for Misha, but then he solved the problem brilliantly. Head up, tail loosely high like a banner of self-confidence, he broke into a canter and bounded straight for the Saint Bernard." For both the woman on the dark street and for Misha, successful resolutions to their problems emerged from instinctual action plans.

History of success or failure. Whether or not we are able to use these instinctual action plans is greatly influenced by our past successes and failures in similar situations.

Causes of Trauma

I have been amazed at the broad range of traumatic events and reactions I have observed throughout my career. Some, like childhood surgeries, are significant but seemingly benign events in the person's memory. A client describes the following formative childhood experience at age four:

> I struggled with masked giants who were strapping me to a high, white table. Silhouetted in the cold, harsh light that glared in my eyes was the figure of someone coming towards me with a black mask. The mask had a vile smell that caused me to choke and I continued to struggle as it was forced down onto my face. Trying desperately to scream and turn away, I spun into a dizzying, black tunnel of horrific hallucinations. I awoke in a gray-green room, devastated. Except for a very bad sore throat, it appeared that I was perfectly okay. I was not.
>
> I felt utterly and completely abandoned and betrayed. All that I had been told was that I could have my favorite ice cream and that my parents would be with me. After the operation I lost the sense of a safe, comprehensible world where I had the ability to respond. I became consumed by a helpless sense of shame and a feeling that I was bad" [the rational brain assumes that

he must be bad to deserve this kind of punishment]. For years after this annihilating experience, I feared bedtime and would sometimes wake up in the middle of the night. Gasping for breath and too scared and ashamed to cry out, I lay alone, terrified of suffocating to death.

By the age of six or seven, family stress and the pressure of school intensified my symptoms. I was sent to see a child psychiatrist. Her main concern was a shaggy, dirty, white, stuffed dog that I needed to have beside me to fall asleep. The reason for my anxiety and excessive shyness went undiscovered. The doctor's approach was to further frighten me by telling me about the problems needing a stuffed friend would cause me as an adult. I must say that the therapy "worked" in that regard (I threw my dog away). However, my symptoms continued and I developed chronic anxiety attacks, frequent stomachaches, and other "psychosomatic" problems that lasted from junior high into graduate school.

Many events can cause traumatic reactions later in life, depending on how the person experienced them at the time. Some examples of common traumatic antecedents are:

- Fetal trauma (intra-uterine)
- Birth trauma
- Loss of a parent or close family member
- Illness, high fevers, accidental poisoning
- Physical injuries, including falls and accidents
- Sexual, physical, and emotional abuse, including severe abandonment, or beatings
- Witnessing violence
- Natural disasters such as earthquakes, fires, and floods
- Certain medical and dental procedures
- Surgery, particularly tonsillectomies with ether; operations for ear problems and for so-called "lazy eye"

- Anesthesia
- Prolonged immobilization; the casting and splinting of young children's legs or torsos for various reasons (turned-in feet, scoliosis)

The fact that hospitalizations and medical procedures routinely produce traumatic results comes as a surprise to many people. The traumatic aftereffects from prolonged immobilization, hospitalizations, and especially surgeries are often long-lasting and severe. Even though a person may recognize that an operation is necessary, and despite the fact that they are unconscious as the surgeon cuts through flesh, muscle, and bone, it still registers in the body as a life-threatening event. On the "cellular level" the body perceives that it has sustained a wound serious enough to place it in mortal danger. Intellectually, we may believe in an operation, but on a primal level, our bodies do not. Where trauma is concerned, the perception of the instinctual nervous system carries more weight—much more. This biological fact is a primary reason why surgery will often produce a post-traumatic reaction.

In an "ordinary" story from the July, 1993 edition of *Reader's Digest* entitled "Everything is not Okay," a father describes his son Robbie's "minor" knee surgery:

> The doctor tells me that everything is okay. The knee is fine, but everything is not okay for the boy waking up in a drug-induced nightmare, thrashing around on his hospital bed—a sweet boy who never hurt anybody, staring out from his anesthetic haze with the eyes of a wild animal, striking the nurse, screaming "Am I alive?" and forcing me to grab his arms...staring right into my eyes and not knowing who I am.

The boy is taken home, but his fear continues. He awakes fitfully..."only to try to vomit and I [the father] go crazy trying to be useful, so I do what you do in the suburban United States—buy your kid a toy so that you'll feel better."

Millions of parents are left feeling helpless, unable to understand the dramatic (or subtle) changes in their children's behavior following a wide range of traumatic events. In Section Four we will discuss how to prevent these reactions from occurring, both in adults and children.

In a real sense all life is inter-related. All men are
caught in an inescapable network of mutuality, tied in
a single garment of destiny. Whatever affects one direct-
ly affects all indirectly. I can never be what I ought to
be until you are what you ought to be, and you can never
be what you ought to be until I am what I ought to be.
This is the inter-related structure of reality.
—Rev. Martin Luther King, Jr.

5

Healing and Community

Shamanic Approaches to Healing

Throughout recorded and oral history, it has been the task of the shaman, or tribal healer, to help restore balance and health in individuals and communities where it has been disrupted. In contrast to Western medicine, which has taken its time in recognizing the debilitating impacts of trauma, shamanistic cultures have acknowledged such wounds for a very long time. Shamanistic cultures view illness and trauma as a problem for the entire community, not just for the individual or individuals who manifest the symptoms. Consequently, people in these societies seek healing as much for the good of the whole as for themselves. This approach has special applications in the transformation of trauma in our society today. While this endorsement is not intended to suggest that we all seek shamanistic aid in healing trauma, we can gain valuable insight by studying how shamans address traumatic reactions.

The methods used over the ages by medicine men and women are varied and complex. However, these diverse rituals and beliefs share a common understanding of trauma. When people are overwhelmed, their "souls" may become separated from their bodies. According to Mircea Eliade[5] (an important scholar of shamanistic practice), "rape of the soul" is by far the most widespread and damaging cause of illness cited by shamanic healers. Missing important parts of their souls, people become lost in states of spiritual suspension. From the shamanistic point of view, illness is a result of being stuck in "spiritual limbo."

Since pre-civilization, shamanistic healers from many cultures have been able to successfully orchestrate the conditions that encourage the "lost soul" to return to its rightful place in the body. Through colorful rituals, these so-called "primitive" healers catalyze powerful innate healing forces in their patients. An atmosphere of community support enhanced by drumming, chanting, dancing, and trancing creates the environment in which this healing takes place. Often the proceedings continue for days and may involve the use of plant substances and other pharmacological catalysts. Significantly, while the ceremonies themselves vary, the beneficiary of the healing almost always shakes and trembles as the event nears its conclusion. This is the same phenomenon that occurs in all animals when they release bound-up energy. It happened with Nancy that day more than twenty-five years ago in my urban office.

Although we are cultures apart from these primitive peoples, modernized trauma survivors often use similar language to describe their experiences. "My father stole my soul when he had sex with me" is a typical description of the devastating loss experienced by the individual who was sexually abused as a child. When people share how they feel after medical procedures and operations, they also convey this sense of loss and disconnection. I have heard many women say, "The pelvic exam felt like

---

[5]Shamanism—Princeton University Press, 2nd Printing, 1974

a rape of my body and spirit." People often feel disembodied for months or years following surgery employing general anesthesia. The same results can appear after seemingly minor accidents, falls, and even deep betrayals and abandonment. Although we don't have the language for it, many of us sense traumatic injury at the soul level. Rod Steiger, in a poignant interview with Oprah Winfrey, describes his decades-long depression that started after he had surgery: "I began going slowly into a greasy, yellow, jelly fog that permeated into my body...into my heart, my spirit, and my soul...It took me over, robbing me of my life."

In shamanistic medicine, since disease is attributed to the soul having strayed, been stolen, or otherwise dislocated, treatments attempt to capture it or "oblige it to resume its place in the patient's body." Only the shaman, according to Eliade, "sees" the spirits and knows how to exorcise them. "Only he recognizes that the soul has fled and only he is able to overtake it in ecstasy and return it to its body." In nearly all of the "soul retrievals" described by Eliade, shamans heal their patients by interceding in the spirit realm. He describes a Toleut shaman calling back the soul of a sick child: "Come back to your country; to your people...to the Yurt, by the bright fire!... Come back to your father... to your mother..."[6]

A crucial parameter in the healing of trauma is reflected in this simple poetry. The welcoming support of friends, relatives, families, or tribal members is needed to coax the spirit back into the traumatized body. This event is often ritualized and experienced as a group celebration. Shamanism recognizes that deep interconnection, support, and social cohesion are necessary requirements in the healing of trauma. Each of us must take the responsibility for healing our own traumatic injuries.

---

[6]Ibid.

We must do this for ourselves, for our families, and for the society at large. In acknowledging our need for connection with one another, we must enlist the support of our communities in this recovery process.

Physicians and mental health workers today don't speak of retrieving souls, but they are faced with a similar task—restoring wholeness to an organism that has been fragmented by trauma. Shamanistic concepts and procedures treat trauma by uniting lost soul and body in the presence of community. This approach is alien to the technological mind. However, these procedures do seem to succeed where conventional Western approaches fail. My conclusion is that significant aspects of shamanic practice are valid. When it comes to trauma, we have much to learn from the ways these traditional people practice their medicine. After the 1994 Los Angeles earthquake, it was those families (often from Third World countries) who camped, ate, and played together that fared better than many middle-class families. Those who remained isolated—obsessively watching replays of the disaster, listening to interviews with geologists claiming "the big one is yet to come"—were much more susceptible to traumatic effects than those who supported each other in community.

Several of my colleagues from Los Angeles reported that ornamental carp (large goldfish) in their garden ponds formed into tight groups some hours before the earthquake. They remained that way for several hours afterwards. I was told a similar story by Nancy Harvey, a consulting ethologist for the San Diego Wildlife Park. I asked Nancy whether the animals exhibited trauma-like symptoms after the fierce southern California fire burned right up to the edge of the antelope habitat. She said that they hadn't, and described a curious behavior in which the impala and other antelope populations formed groups away from the fences, and remained together until the fire was extinguished.

Somatic Experiencing®

While I recognize the shamanic approach as valid, and am grateful for what I have learned while working and teaching with shamans from several different cultures, the Somatic Experiencing approach presented in this book is not shamanic. One important difference, I believe, is that each of us has a greater capacity to heal ourselves than the shamanic approach would suggest. We can do much to retrieve our own souls. With the support of friends and relatives, we gain a powerful resource for our healing journeys.

This section includes exercises designed to help you heal trauma in yourself and others. Obviously, a trained professional is beneficial for guiding the process, particularly if the trauma took place at an early age, or abuse and betrayal occurred. However, even without professional assistance these exercises can be very powerful when practiced alone, in pairs, or in groups. Keep in mind that denial can be a powerful force. *A word of warning: doing these exercises can activate traumatic symptoms. If you feel overwhelmed or consistently stuck, please seek professional help.*

In the shamanic approach, the medicine man or woman calls for the spirit to return to the body. In Somatic Experiencing, you initiate your own healing by re-integrating lost or fragmented portions of your essential self. In order to accomplish this task, you need a strong desire to become whole again. This desire will serve as an anchor through which your soul can reconnect to your body. Healing will take place as formerly frozen elements of your experience (in the form of symptoms) are released from their trauma-serving tasks, enabling you to gradually thaw. When you thaw, you have the possibility to become more fluid and functional.

Acknowledging the Need to Heal

Cultures that use ritual and shamans to heal trauma may seem primitive and superstitious, but they have one important advantage—they address the problem directly. These cultures openly acknowledge the need to heal when someone in their community has been overwhelmed. Most modern cultures, including ours, fall victim to the prevailing attitude that strength means endurance; that it is somehow heroic to be able to carry on regardless of the severity of our symptoms. A majority of us accept this social custom without question. Using the power of the neo-cortex, our ability to rationalize, it is possible to give the impression that one has come through a severely threatening event, even a war, with "nary a scratch"; and that's exactly what many of us do. We carry on with a "stiff upper lip," much to the admiration of others—heroes, as if nothing had happened at all.

By encouraging us to be superhuman, these social mores do great injustice to the individual and the society. If we attempt to move ahead with our lives, without first yielding to the gentler urges that will guide us back through these harrowing experiences, then our show of strength becomes little more than illusion. In the meantime, the traumatic effects will grow steadily more severe, firmly entrenched, and chronic. The incomplete responses now frozen in our nervous systems are like indestructible time bombs, primed to go off when aroused by force. Until human beings can find the appropriate tools and the support necessary to dismantle this force, we will continue to have unexplained blowups. Real heroism comes from having the courage to openly acknowledge one's experiences, not from suppressing or denying them.

Let Us Begin—Calling the Spirit Back to the Body

The disconnection between body and soul is one of the most important effects of trauma. Loss of skin sensation is a common physical manifestation of the numbness and disconnection people experience after trauma. To begin to recover sensation, the following awareness exercise will be useful throughout the mending process. The initial cost of $15 to $40 for a pulsing shower head is well worth the investment.

Exercise

For ten minutes or so each day, take a gentle, pulsing shower in the following way: at a cool or slightly warm temperature setting, expose your entire body to the pulsing water. Put your full awareness into the region of your body where the rhythmical stimulation is focused. Let your consciousness move to each part of your body as you rotate. Hold the backs of your hands to the shower head; then the palms and wrists; then both sides of your face, shoulders, underarms, etc. Be sure to include every part of your body: head, forehead, neck, chest, back, legs, pelvis, hips, thighs, ankles, and feet. Pay attention to the sensation in each area, even if it feels blank, numb, or painful. While you are doing this, say "this is my head, neck," etc. "I welcome you back." Another similar awakening is to gently slap the different parts of your body briskly. Again, this will help re-establish a sense of a body with skin sensation when done regularly over time.

This simple exercise will begin to welcome the soul back

to the body. It's an important first step toward bridging the split between body, mind, and spirit that often occurs in the wake of trauma.

My belief is in the blood and flesh as being wiser than the intellect. The body-unconscious is where life bubbles up in us. It is how we know that we are alive, alive to the depths of our souls and in touch somewhere with the vivid reaches of the cosmos.
—D.H. Lawrence

6

In Trauma's Reflection

Medusa

In this chapter we begin to explore a general approach to mastering trauma. In being able to experience ourselves as sensing human animals we can begin to loosen trauma's grip on us and to transform its powerful energies. We don't confront it directly, however, or we could find ourselves seized in its frightening grip. Like a Chinese finger trap, we must gently slide into trauma and then draw ourselves gradually out.

In the myth of Medusa, anyone who looked directly into her eyes would quickly turn to stone. Such is the case with trauma. If we attempt to confront trauma head on, it will continue to do what it has already done—immobilize us in fear. Before Perseus set out to conquer Medusa, he was warned by Athena not to look directly at the Gorgon. Heeding the goddess's wisdom, he used his shield to reflect Medusa's image; by doing so, he was able to cut off her head. Likewise, the solution to vanquishing trauma comes not through confronting it directly, but by working with its reflection, mirrored in our instinctual responses.

65

Trauma is so arresting that traumatized people will focus on it compulsively. Unfortunately, the situation that defeated them once will defeat them again and again. Body sensations can serve as a guide to reflect where we are experiencing trauma, and to lead us to our instinctual resources. These resources give us the power to protect ourselves from predators and other hostile forces. Each of us possesses these instinctual resources. Once we learn how to access them we can create our own shields to reflect and heal our traumas.

In dreams, mythical stories, and lore, one universal symbol for the human body and its instinctual nature is the horse. Interestingly enough, when Medusa was slain, two things emerged from her body: Pegasus, the winged horse, and Chrysaor, a warrior with a golden sword. We couldn't find a more appropriate metaphor. The sword symbolizes absolute truth, the mythic heros ultimate weapon of defense. It conveys a sense of clarity and triumph, of rising to meet extraordinary challenges, and of ultimate resourcefulness. The horse symbolizes instinctual grounding, while wings create an image of movement, soaring, and rising above an earth-bound existence. Since the horse represents instinct and body, the winged horse speaks of transformation through embodiment. Together the winged horse and the golden sword are auspicious symbols for the resources traumatized people discover in the process of vanquishing their own Medusas.

As we begin the healing process we use what is known as the "felt sense," or internal body sensations. These sensations serve as a portal through which we find the symptoms, or reflections of trauma. In directing our attention to these internal body sensations, rather than attacking the trauma head-on, we can unbind and free the energies that have been held in check.

The Felt Sense

Our feelings and our bodies are like water
flowing into water. We learn to swim within the
energies of the (body) senses.
—Tarthang Tulku

Just as Perseus used his shield to confront Medusa, so may traumatized people use their shield-equivalent of sensation, or the "felt sense," to master trauma. The felt sense encompasses the clarity, instinctual power, and fluidity necessary to transform trauma.

According to Eugene Gendlin, who coined the term "felt sense" in his book *Focusing*[7]:

> A felt sense is not a mental experience but a physical one. *Physical*. A bodily awareness of a situation or person or event. An internal aura that encompasses everything you feel and know about the given subject at a given time—encompasses it and communicates it to you all at once rather than detail by detail.

The felt sense is a difficult concept to define with words, as language is a linear process and the felt sense is a non-linear experience. Consequently, dimensions of meaning are lost in the attempt to articulate this experience.

We define an "organism" as a complex structure of interdependent and subordinate elements whose relation and properties are largely determined by their functions in the whole. Therefore, the whole of the organism is greater than the sum of its individual parts. In a similar way, the felt sense unifies a great deal of scattered data and gives it meaning. For example, when we see a beautiful image on television, what we are seeing is a vast array of digitized dots called pixels. If we were to focus on the individual elements (pixels), we would see dots and not the beautiful image. Likewise, in hearing your favorite musical score you do not focus on the indi-

---

[7] Focusing—Bantam Books, 1981

vidual notes, but rather on the total aural experience. Your experience is much greater than the sum of the individual notes.

The felt sense can be said to be the medium through which we experience the totality of sensation. In the process of healing trauma, we focus on the individual sensations (like television pixels or melodic notes). When observed both closely and from a distance, these sensations are simultaneously experienced as foreground and background, creating a gestalt, or integration of experience.

Every event can be experienced both in its duality, as individual parts, and as a unified whole. Those which are perceived in a unified manner through the felt sense can bring revelations about how to undo the trauma. To harness the instincts necessary to heal trauma, we must be able to identify and employ the indicators of trauma that are made available to us through the felt sense.

Exercise

Following is an exercise that will begin to give you a basic, experiential understanding of the felt sense. Wherever you are as you read this, make yourself as comfortable as possible.

Feel the way your body makes contact with the surface that is supporting you.

Sense into your skin and notice the way your clothes feel.

Sense underneath your skin—what sensations are there?

Now, gently remembering these sensations, how do you know that you feel comfortable? What physical sensations contribute to the overall feeling of comfort?

Does becoming more aware of these sensations make you feel more or less comfortable? Does this change over time?

Sit for a moment and enjoy the felt sense of feeling comfortable.
Good!

Being consciously aware of your body and its sensations makes any experience more intense. It is important to recognize that the experience of comfort comes from your felt sense of comfort and not from the chair, the sofa, or whatever surface you are sitting on. As a visit to any furniture store will soon reveal, you can't know that a chair is comfortable until you sit on it and get a bodily sense of what it feels like.

The felt sense blends together most of the information that forms your experience. Even when you are not consciously aware of it, the felt sense is telling you where you are and how you feel at any given moment. It is relaying the overall experience of the organism, rather than interpreting what is happening from the standpoint of the individual parts. Perhaps the best way to describe the felt sense is to say that it is the experience of being in a living body that understands the nuances of its environment by way of its responses to that environment.

In many ways, the felt sense is like a stream moving through an ever-changing landscape. It alters its character in resonance with its surroundings. When the land is rugged and steep, the stream moves with vigor and energy, swirling and bubbling as it crashes over rocks and debris. Out on the plains, the stream meanders so slowly that one might wonder whether it is moving at all. Rains and spring thaw can rapidly increase its volume, possibly even flood nearby land. In the same way, once the setting has been interpreted and defined by the felt sense, we will blend into whatever conditions we find ourselves. This amazing sense encompasses both the content and climate of our internal and external environments. Like the stream, it shapes itself to fit those environments.

The physical (external) senses of sight, sound, smell, touch, and taste are elements that contribute only a portion of the information that builds the foundation for the felt sense. Other important data are derived from our body's internal awareness (the positions it takes, the tensions it has, the movements it makes, temperature, etc.). The felt sense can be influenced—even changed by our thoughts—yet it's not a thought, it's something we feel. Emotions contribute to the felt sense, but they play a less important role than most people believe. "Categorical" emotions such as sorrow, anger, fear, disgust, and joy are intense and direct. There is a limited variety of these types of feelings and they are easily recognized and named. This is not so with the felt sense.

The felt sense encompasses a complex array of ever-shifting nuances. The feelings we experience are typically much more subtle, complex, and intricate than what we can convey in language. As you read the following phrases, imagine how much more you might feel than is expressed: Looking at a mountain peak bathed in an alpine glow; seeing a blue summer sky dotted with soft white clouds; going to a ball game and dripping mustard on your shirt; feeling the ocean spray as the surf crashes onto rock and cliff; touching an opening rose or a blade of grass topped with a drop of morning dew; listening to a Brahms concerto; watching a group of brightly dressed children singing ethnic folk songs; walking along a country road; or enjoying time with a friend. You can imagine going through a day without emotion, but to live in the absence of the felt sense is not just unthinkable, it is impossible. To live without the felt sense violates the most basic experience of being alive.

The felt sense is sometimes vague, always complex,

and ever-changing. It moves, shifts, and transforms constantly. It can vary in intensity and clarity, enabling us to shift our perceptions. It does this by giving us the process as well as what is needed for change. Through the felt sense we are able to move, to acquire new information, to interrelate with one another and, ultimately, to know who we are. It is so integral to our experience of being human that we take it for granted, sometimes to the point of not even realizing that it exists until we deliberately attend to it.

Although I have become much more aware of my own body sensations, I find I need a process to move into the felt sense, as you will see from the following account of a typical day in the life of Peter.

I return home from a busy day of errands in town and immediately reach for the TV remote. Before I push the button I remind myself to stop this habitual distraction and look inside. At first I am aware of racing thoughts. They are like swarming flies. I let that unpleasant quality permeate my consciousness. The buzzing intensifies and my awareness shifts to a tenseness throughout my body—particularly in my chest. After a while, I begin to notice areas of discomfort and pain—they seem to move around. I notice my thoughts slowing a bit as I take a fuller, easier breath. I see some fleeting images of the day's events. More time passes and I experience a pain building in the back of my head. I feel restless—jittery in my arms and legs. I think about getting up and busying myself. Instead I stay seated. Before long I notice my head wanting to nod forward. This becomes a rhythmic, gentle, rocking motion. I notice a warmth in my hands and, as they begin to tingle mildly, I realize how cold they have been. I sense a slight warmth in my belly, which I attend to as it intensifies and spreads. The telephone starts ringing in rapid sequence—I feel jangled and annoyed. There is a restless sensation in my arms that subsides as I notice birds singing outside the window. The next thing that comes into my awareness is the image of an old friend. I experience a warm feeling as I recognize him. I notice a sensation in my chest of spaciousness. It has a full and round quality. I experience this "felt image" of my friend within that spaciousness. I attach the word "gladness," feeling a calm, soft, pulsing flow into my arms and legs and I am glad (i.e., I have the felt sense of gladness).

Let the Body Speak Its Mind

There are many reasons why we might choose to develop a greater facility with the felt sense. It heightens our enjoyment of sensual experiences. It can be a doorway to spiritual states. Studies (reported by Gendlin in *Focusing*) have shown that therapies employing the felt sense are generally more effective than those that don't. The felt sense helps people feel more natural—more grounded, more at home in their bodies. It can enhance our sense of balance and coordination. It improves memory and provides us deeper access to the subtle instinctual impulses that guide the healing of trauma. It increases creativity. It is from the felt sense that we experience well-being, peace, and connectedness. It is how we experience the "self."

Nowadays the phrase "trust your gut" is used commonly. The felt sense is the means through which you can learn to hear this instinctual voice. Most of us have little experience to help guide us to this awareness. We are used to living in a very disconnected way—a way that hasn't embraced our felt sense. If you are one of these people, contacting the felt sense is probably going to be unfamiliar. Don't be discouraged. It's difficult at first but hang in there; it will come. Western culture does not teach us to experience ourselves in this way. We are taught to read, write, calculate, etc., but rarely do we come across a school that teaches anything about the felt sense. It never gets mentioned at home, on the street, or anywhere else, for that matter. Most people use this sense every day, but very few of us consciously acknowledge it, and even fewer cultivate it. It is important to remember that the felt sense is a wonderful and very natural human capacity.

Those of us who are traumatized should be aware that learning to work with the felt sense may be challenging. Part of the dynamic of trauma is that it cuts us off from our internal experience as a way of protecting our organisms from sensations and emotions that could be overwhelming. It may take you a while to trust enough to allow a little internal experience to come through. Be patient and keep reminding yourself that you don't need to experience everything now. This hero's journey proceeds one tiny step at a time.

Using the Felt Sense to Listen to the Organism

We want to begin to tap into our instinctual voices. The first step is learning to use the felt sense to listen to that voice. The most helpful attribute in this journey is gentleness. Contacting the instinctual self is powerful stuff. Never try to force it. Take it easy, take it slow. If you feel overwhelmed at any time, you may have overdone it. The next time you come to that curve, slow down. This is definitely one time that you will get there faster by going slower. Sometimes, the felt sense appears slowly; other times you are hit by a flash of understanding and the whole thing becomes clear to you in an instant. The best approach is to maintain an open and curious attitude.

Don't try to interpret, analyze, or explain what is happening; just experience and note it. It is also unnecessary to dredge up memories, emotions, insights, or anything else, for that matter. If they come that's fine, but it is more important to observe them without interpretation or emotional attachment; observe them and let them go. "Take it as it comes" is the best way to learn the language of your felt sense. Information will come to you in the form of words, pictures, insights, and emotions, which invariably will be accompanied by another layer of sensations. These sensations can be elusive yet recognizable when you learn how to pay attention on a very subtle level.

Learning to know yourself through the felt sense is a first step toward healing trauma. Earlier, I described this sense as a stream. As you develop your ability to pay attention to the felt sense, you will see that this is an extremely appropriate analogy. Reactions and responses to the people, objects, and situations you encounter begin to move through your awareness like an ever-changing stream. The exercise that follows is an in-depth version of the earlier exercise using the felt sense. It will help give you a sense of what this "stream" is like. It will also help you develop your ability to listen to what the organism as a whole has to say.

Exercise

To do this exercise you will need a book or magazine with lots of pictures. Coffee table books, nature or travel magazines, and illustrated calendars work well. You don't want to do anything but look at pictures for this exercise. Reading uses a different part of the brain than the part that senses. In this exercise you want to emphasize direct perception.

Before opening the book, sense your arms and legs and

notice the sensations where they make contact with the surface that supports you. Next, add any other physical sensations you may be experiencing such as the feel of your clothes, shoes, or hair. Finally, add any other sensations you feel such as tightness, openness, temperature, tingling, shaking, hunger, thirst, sleepiness, etc. Return to the felt sense throughout the exercise to bring your awareness more completely into your body and breath.

Look at the first picture. Notice how you respond to it. Do you like it, feel neutral about it, dislike it? Is it beautiful, calming, strange, mysterious, haunting, joyful, sad, artistic, or something else? Whatever your response is, just notice it. If there are several parts to your response, notice what they are. This is normal. We hardly ever have just one reaction to anything.

Now ask yourself: **How** *do I know that this is my response to this picture? Try to identify the bodily sensations that accompany your viewing of the picture. Some of the sensations may be subtle, others will be stronger. Whatever they are, just notice them. Do you feel "energy" move or suddenly stop? If you feel energy move, how does it move, slowly, fast, in what direction? Is there some kind of rhythm to the sensation? Is it located in any particular part of your body? Does it feel tense, loose, easy, relaxed, tingling, heavy, light, cool, dense, warm, invigorating, or something else? Pay attention to your breathing and your heartbeat. Notice how your skin feels, and how your body feels overall. Experiencing any one of these sensations is a beginning point.*

Stay with the sensations for a few minutes and see if they change. They may stay the same, disappear, become stronger or weaker, or change to something else. Notice these dynamics. Whatever happens, just notice it. If the sensations become uncomfortable, just shift your attention elsewhere for a moment.

Turn to the next picture and repeat the process. As you become more familiar with this process, you can move through the book or magazine at a speed that is comfortable for you. When first learning to use the felt sense, you may find it is easier to access when you move slowly, focusing mainly on sensing and sensation.

Later on, I introduce exercises that work specifically with the physical and emotional sensations related to trauma. Since certain emotions become enmeshed with traumatic symptoms, it is necessary to learn how to explore them. Also, because emotions can be powerful, compelling, dramatic, and intriguing, they present a special challenge for working with the felt sense. Most people find emotions a far more interesting topic of investigation than mere sensations. However, if you want to learn to use the felt sense, and especially if you want to learn to use the felt sense to resolve trauma, you must learn how to recognize the physiological manifestations (sensations) that underlie your emotional reactions. Sensations come from symptoms, and symptoms come from compressed energy; that energy is what we have to work with in this process. Through sensation and the felt sense, this vast energy can gradually be decompressed and harnessed for the purpose of transforming trauma.

Again, remember to be gentle, to take it slow and easy, and don't attach any kind of interpretation or judgment to what you experience. Just let whatever you experience move you through to the next experience. Even though the exercise may seem familiar to you, try to approach it freshly, as though you've never done anything like it before—you will get more out of it.

Exercise

Instead of using a book or magazine for this exercise, you will be using photographs and memorabilia. A family photo album, or a scrapbook containing memorabilia from a trip or an earlier period in your life is perfect. Any pictures should be mostly of people you know fairly well and places you have visited. Again, you don't want to do anything but look at pictures for this exercise.

Begin by sensing your arms and legs and notice what you feel where the limbs make contact with the surface that supports you. Add any other physical sensations you may be experiencing. Doing this every once in a while throughout the exercise will help you bring your awareness more completely into your body.

Turn to the first picture (or the first page, if you are using a scrapbook). Notice how you respond to it. What emotions does it evoke? Do you feel happy, amused, apprehensive, vaguely upset, confused, sad, angry, loving, grateful, embarrassed, hateful, annoyed, disgusted, simply nostalgic, or something else? All of these emotions feel different. They are all experienced differently. Whatever your reaction is, just notice it. If there are several reactions, notice what they are. Is your reaction strong or mild? How do you know that it is strong or mild? If you can answer this question in terms of sensations in your body, you are on your way to being able to use the physiological undercurrent of emotion.

Now, ask yourself: How do I know that this is my emotional reaction to this picture? Try to identify the sensations that underlie your reaction to the picture. Some of the sensations may be strong and others more subtle. Whatever they are, just notice them. Do you feel any kind of tension or energy? If so, how much of it is there and where is it? Pay attention to your breathing, your heartbeat, and to tension patterns throughout your body. Notice how your skin feels. How does your body feel overall? Does your reaction feel tense, powerful, fuzzy, smooth, jagged, tangled, numb, hot, loose, sticky, relaxed, heavy, light, cool, dense, warm, invigorating, tingling, vibrating, shaking, slimy, solid, or some-

thing else? Where is the feeling in your body? If the sensa-
tion seems to have some bulk, ask yourself what material it
seems to be made out of. If you feel energy move, how does
it move — slow, fast, in what direction? Is there some kind of
swell to the sensation? Where is it located? Be as specific as
you can. How do you know what your reaction is?

If you notice that you are using words that are usually
thought of as emotions, take each one and ask yourself:
How do I know that I feel emotion? Because emotions are
based on connections with the past, the picture or memora-
bilia may bring memories of other events. Just notice the
sensations that come with these memories in the same way.
Keep reminding yourself to sense and to describe what you
sense as sensations, not as emotions or thoughts.

Turn to the next picture and repeat the process.
Remember to go slowly enough to be able to notice the sen-
sations that arise in response to the pictures. For each pic-
ture or page of your scrapbook, stay with the sensations that
are evoked for a few minutes and see if they change. They
may stay the same or disappear, but they may also become
stronger. Whatever happens, just notice it.

If the feelings or sensations become too intense or
unpleasant, deliberately shift your attention to a pleasant
experience that you have had, or that you can imagine hav-
ing. Focus all your awareness on the bodily felt sensations of
that experience instead. Shifting your attention to the other
sensations will help the intensity of the uncomfortable feel-
ing to subside. Remember that unresolved trauma can be a
powerful force. If you continue to feel overwhelmed by the
exercises or any of the material in the book, please stop for
now, try again later, or, enlist the support of a trained pro-
fessional.

If an image of a horrifying scene shows up in your
mind's eye, ever so gently notice what sensations come
with it. Sometimes, when sensations are intense, images

come first. The sensation is ultimately what will help you move through the trauma—whatever it is. You may end up knowing what it is and you may not. For now, just be reassured that as you move through your reactions, the need to know whether it was real or not will loosen its grip. If there is an objective need to know whether it is true, such as to protect a child who may be at risk, you will be in a better position to handle the situation effectively.

Be aware that the energies of trauma can be bound up in *beliefs* about being raped or abused. By challenging these beliefs, especially if they aren't true, some of that energy may be released. If this is the case for you, rest and give yourself plenty of time to process this new information. Stay with the sensations you experience as much as possible, and don't be alarmed if you feel tremulous or weak. Both are evidence that normal discharge is happening. Don't force yourself to do more than you can handle. If you feel tired, take a nap or go to bed early. Part of the grace of the nervous system is that it is constantly self-regulating. What you can't process today will be available to be processed some other time when you are stronger, more resourceful, and better able to do it.

There are both physiological and psychological elements of the felt sense. I've outlined some of their key differences in the following two subsections. The first subsection focuses on how the organism communicates through its physiology; the second focuses on some of the psychological conventions and customs from which the organism operates. Ideally, these discussions will help you strengthen your ability to use the felt sense in the land of physiology and sensation.

How the Organism Communicates

The organism has its own way of communicating, which

you'll learn more about as you continue to read this book. A couple of very important characteristics of how it communicates will already be evident from the exercises above. Think back to the last exercise. Did you notice that when you described sensations, you used words that referred to physiological sensations that were familiar to you? If you have never felt something that is fuzzy, you won't know what fuzzy is and the organism wouldn't use fuzzy to describe a sensation. The organism uses what it already knows to describe what it is experiencing. Don't take it literally. A sensation can feel like it is fuzzy, jagged, made of glass, wood, or plastic. Obviously, "feel like" is a key part of the description. There isn't anything inside you that is really fuzzy or jagged. You don't have pieces of wood, glass, or plastic inside you, unless you have suffered some very poorly executed surgical procedures. The sensations just feel like these things. They are metaphors. Sensations, however, can also be literal and correspond with information received from organs, bones, and muscles.

The organism doesn't just use characteristics of physical objects to communicate. It also uses images that can easily be construed as memories. The energetic forces that result in trauma are immensely powerful. The emotions that are generated by trauma include rage, terror, and helplessness. If your body elects to communicate the presence of such energies to you through images—consider the kinds of images you might see. The possibilities are endless. They will have one thing in common—they won't be pretty. One mistake that is made all too often is that people interpret these visual communications as reality. A traumatized individual may end up believing that he or she was raped or tortured when the actual message the organism is trying to convey is that this sensation you are experiencing *feels* like rape or torture. The actual culprit could just as easily have been a terrifying medical procedure, an automobile accident, or even childhood neglect. It could literally be anything.

Of course, some images really are memories. People who have suffered from rape or torture will draw on those experiences in producing images. It is common for children who have had these experiences not to remember them until years later. Even if the images are "true" memories, we have to understand their role in healing. The explanations, beliefs, and interpretations connected with memories can get in the way of completely entering and deepening the felt sense. The sensations that accompany these images are immensely valuable. For our purposes, what matters most is how the sensations feel and how they change.

Sensation and the Felt Sense

When working with physiology, the first thing to recognize is that the felt sense is closely related to awareness. Its like watching the scenery, or in this case, sensing the scenery. Awareness means experiencing what is present without trying to change or interpret it. Anytime you catch yourself saying or thinking, "this means—," you are attaching an interpretation to your experience that will take you out of simple awareness and back into the realm of psychology. Meaning does have a place in healing trauma as a consequence of direct awareness. For now, it is more important to focus on what you experience rather than on what you think about it. I'll say more about the importance of meaning in healing trauma later.

Sensations are the physical phenomena that contribute to our overall experience. Pick up an ice cube, for instance. Some of the sensations that contribute to how an ice cube feels include: cold, smooth, hard, and cube-shaped. All of these are important in creating a complete understanding of the ice cube. The same is true of internal sensations. When you are first starting out, it is especially important to check and double-check that you have brought every characteristic of a particular sensation into your awareness by consciously making note of it. You can miss some characteristics of a sensation because you take them for granted, because you aren't letting the whole sensation into your awareness, or because the characteristic in question is subtle or elusive.

An ice cube straight from the freezer can be sticky, as well as cold, hard, smooth, and cube-shaped. After a short while, it will be wet instead of sticky. First sticky, then wet helps complete the picture of the cold, hard, smooth, cube-shaped thing. Apply the analogy to an internal experience and, like the ice cube, it will change as you hold it for a while. Once you become aware of them, internal sensations almost always transform into something else. Any change of this sort is usually moving in the direction of a free-flow of energy and vitality.

Rhythm: All Gods Children Got It

You can't push the river.
—Unknown

Sensations occur in infinite variety. This is one of the reasons that simple awareness is so important. Receptivity will help you notice the nuances in your sensations much more easily. In the land of physiology, subtle sensations and rhythms are just as important as blatantly obvious ones.

The last characteristic of the felt sense that I'd like to mention has to do with the importance of rhythm.

Physiological phenomena occur in cycles. These biological rhythms are fundamentally important in the transformation of trauma. It may be difficult at first to have the patience to allow them to come into consciousness. Their pace is much slower than the pace at which most of us live our lives. This is one of the reasons that trauma develops in the first place; we don't give our natural biological rhythms the time they need to reach completion. In most cases, the cycles I'm talking about will run their course in a few minutes at most, but those few minutes are essential. The primary place you will notice these rhythms is in the ebb and flow of your sensations. A sensation will transform into something else (another sensation, image, or a feeling) as you notice all its characteristics and will do so at its own pace—you can't push the river. Becoming attuned to these rhythms and honoring them is part of this process.

You now have the basics for using the felt sense. Think of it as a tool that can help you get to know yourself as a complex, biological and spiritual organism. The felt sense is simple and elegant. Yet, it is billions of times more sophisticated than the most powerful computers. It consists of awareness, sensation, subtlety, variety, and rhythm. If you are beginning to catch on to both its primitive and refined elements, you are right on track.

I contend that the uniqueness of man cannot be seen in all its imposing grandeur unless it is set off against the background of those ancient historical characteristics which man still shares with animal life today.
—Konrad Lorenz

The lively world of our emotions, fears and responses is like a great forest with its fauna. We experience those feelings as though they were wild animals bolting through the foliage of our thick being, timidly peering out in alarm or slyly slinking and cunningly stalking, linking us to our unknown selves...
—Paul Shepard

7

The Animal Experience

The foundation for human physiology evolved with the earliest creatures that crawled out of the primordial ooze. As much as we would like to think otherwise, our connection to that beginning has remained fundamentally the same. At the level of the basic biological organism there isn't any thinking or conceptualizing, there is only instinctual response to whatever presents itself. In the human organism, some of these impulses are obscure, others are all-powerful and compelling. No matter how highly evolved humans become in terms of our abilities to reason, feel, plan, build, synthesize, analyze, experience, and create, there is no substitute for the subtle, instinctual healing forces we share with our primitive past.

The Animals Do It, Too

Nature has endowed nearly all living creatures with very similar nervous system responses to the threat of danger. However, of all species, there is only one that routinely develops long-term, traumatic aftereffects—the human. The only time we see similar effects in other animals is when they are domesticated or consistently subjected to stressful conditions in controlled laboratory environments. In these cases they develop acute and chronic traumatic reactions.

This revelation leads to the following questions:

- Since the nervous system response to threat appears to be well designed and functions efficiently in practically all creatures, why is it that humans are unable to take full advantage of this system?
- Do we not know how to access it?
- Are we overriding the system?
- Why are humans readily traumatized?
- What are the animals doing that we aren't?
- How and what can we learn from animals?

In the natural world, the survival responses we've been discussing are normal, healthy, and to the animals advantage. When animals experience life-threatening events, they quickly move beyond the initial shock reaction and recover. Their reactions are time-limited and do not become chronic. Observing this behavior can give us an understanding of our own instinctual ability to successfully overcome trauma. We can also learn more about how not to interfere with our instincts.

The experience of the felt sense gives us a backdrop for reconnecting with the animal in ourselves. Knowing, feeling, and sensing focuses our attention where healing can begin. Nature has not forgotten us, we have forgotten it. A traumatized person's nervous system is not damaged; it is frozen in a kind of suspended animation. Rediscovering the felt sense will bring warmth and vitality to our experiences. This sense is also a gentle, non-threatening way of re-initiating the instinctual processing of energy that was interrupted when the trauma occurred. Completing this process prevents post-traumatic reactions from becoming chronic. We have built-in mechanisms for responding to and moving toward a natural resolution of trauma. Some of these we share with other animals; some are uniquely our own—particularly our highly developed thought and language processes.

Let's move now to a part of the brain that is of significant importance in the discussion of trauma. Embedded deep within the brain of every animal is the reptilian brain. It is the home of the instincts. The only way to consciously access our healing resources is through sensation and the felt sense. Sensation is the language of the reptilian brain. Biologically and physiologically, the reptilian brain is essential to all animals, including humans. It is encoded with the instinctual plans for the behaviors that ensure the survival of the species (self-preservation and reproduction). Involuntary changes that regulate the body's vital functions are controlled from this part of the brain. The reptilian brain is the template from which all higher life has evolved. While its function can be enhanced or seemingly overridden in higher animals, the behaviors that originate in the reptilian core of the brain are the key to unlocking the mystery of trauma. These behaviors are what allow us to experience ourselves as human animals.

When the Reptilian Brain Speaks, Listen!

> *Its not his fault, he said. Oh, sure, Lex said, He practically ate us and its not his fault. Hes a carnivore. He was just doing what he does.*
> — Michael Crichton, Jurassic Park

For the reptile, conscious choice is not an option. Every

behavior, every movement is instinctual. Instinct and instinct alone controls the search for food, shelter, and a suitable mate for procreation. All defensive strategies are genetically programmed into a primitive and highly effective brain. These behaviors are a part of rhythmical cycles over which the reptile has no control. Day by day, season by season, year by year, for hundreds of millions of years, these rituals of life have been repeated. Why? Because they work.

An insect crawls toward a lizard basking on a log. The lizards tongue flicks, the insect is gone. The lizard doesn't stop to consider whether it is hungry. There is no question about whether the insect is clean enough to eat. It doesn't wonder about its calorie count for the day. It simply eats. Just as it sleeps, reproduces, runs away, freezes, fights, etc. The instinct-dominated life is simple. The lizard has nothing to remember, nothing to plan for, nothing to learn—instinct handles it all.

As mammals, the impala and cheetah (Chapter One) have brains that include both a reptilian core and a more elaborate structure known as the limbic brain. The limbic brain exists in all higher animals (including us) and is the primary site of complex emotional and social behaviors lacking in the reptile. These behaviors do not take the place of the instinctual impulses that derive from the reptilian brain, they complement and enhance them. The limbic brain receives impulses from the reptilian core and elaborates on the data. This evolutionary leap gives the mammal more choices than the reptile.

A herd of impala graze, communicate, and flee as one body in part due to the additional information provided by the limbic brain. In addition to their instinctual response to flee, the impala have developed and retain an understanding of their increased survivability as a group (i.e., the young impalas attempt to rejoin the herd when it was threatened—Chapter One). With the limbic brain, emotions evolved. Emotions gave mammals a more highly developed way to store and communicate information, and paved the way towards the evolution of the rational brain.

Our intellect itself evolved out of an instinctual matrix. Instinct defines the parameters that guide each species to form thoughts and develop language. In the healthy human, instinct, emotion, and intellect work together to create the widest range of choices possible in any given situation.

One With Nature

Hanging, swaying, pulsing, the most vulnerable and insubstantial creature, [the jellyfish] has for its defense the violence and power of the whole ocean, to which it has entrusted its going and its will.
—by Ursula Le Guin–*Lathe of Heaven*

An insect crawls within reach of the lizard's tongue and is gone. A herd of impala smell danger and move as one unit toward safety. These examples demonstrate the potential of animals to immediately translate external clues into instinctual responses from within. Animal and environment are one, with no separation between stimulus and response.

No organism more graphically illustrates this attunement than the jellyfish or the amoebae. Pulsing and surging its way through a fluid medium not much different from its own makeup, the amoeba moves as one with its surroundings. The smallest change in its environment generates an immediate response. For example, the amoebae will reorient itself to move toward indicated food, or away from the presence of toxicity. The external signals it receives and the amoeba's response occur as one event. They are virtually synchronous and synonymous.

This type of attunement is critical to the survival of all organisms. Without it, how can we make appropriate and timely responses to both opportunity and danger? The vehicle for that attunement is the body. In humans that experience is expressed through sensation and the felt sense.

Attunement

> *The first track is the end of a string. At the far end, a being is moving; a mystery, dropping a hint about itself every so many feet, telling you more about itself until you can almost see it, even before you come to it.*
> —from *The Tracker* by Tom Brown as told to William Jon Watkins

In today's world most people lack the ability to stay present or tuned-in to the nuances of their internal and external landscapes. However, this type of awareness remains key to the functioning of many native peoples. Consider the experience of a native tracker in the wild.

In order to be tuned-in to his environment the tracker must stay completely attentive to his animal responses and felt sense. By doing so, he not only becomes more aware of his own reactions, but those of his prey. The tracker and the tracked become one. He knows when the animal is sick or wounded, hungry or tired. He knows when it has been hunting or mating, and how long it has slept. He learns from footprints where the animal has taken a drink. From the drift of snow by a bush, he knows where the animal has slept. On the windswept plateau where there is no sign, the tracker uses his sense of "oneness" with the animal to guide him. Instinct tells him where the animal has gone. He and the animal share a common spirit.

Even though the tracker has become keenly attuned to the animal he is tracking, he must also remain aware of all other stimuli (information) in his environment, both internal and external. He may be being tracked or at least watched by other hungry or curious animals. His safety depends on remaining present by employing the felt sense. In this way his finely tuned senses can pick up the slightest sound or movement. Internally, he may be warned of danger by an intangible sense that something isn't quite right. Smells are rich, colors bright and vibrant. Everything is bursting with life. In this state of awareness it is possible to find beauty in what otherwise might be perceived as mundane—a twig, a caterpillar, a drop of dew on a leaf.

While the tracker is attuned to this flow he feels a deep sense of well-being. He is ready to respond, *alert yet relaxed.* Optimally functioning "orienting responses" give the tracker confidence and a sense of security about his ability to successfully identify and meet any challenge he encounters.

For wild animals, these instinctual responses mean survival—offering the capability for attunement and oneness with the environment that will keep them alive. For humans, far more is available through the utilization of these animal responses. They enhance our capacity for connection and enjoyment, bringing aliveness and vitality. When we are healthy and untraumatized, these instinctual responses add sensuality, variety, and a sense of wonder to our lives.

The Orienting Response

The hadosaur continued to eat, just a few feet from him. Grant looked at the two elongated airholes on top of the flat upper bill. Apparently, the dinosaur couldn't smell Grant. And even though the left eye was looking right at him, for some reason the hadosaur didn't react to him. He remembered how the tyrannosaur had failed to see him, the previous night. He decided on an experiment. He coughed. Instantly the hadosaur froze, the big head suddenly still, the jaws no longer chewing. Only the eye moved, looking for the source of the sound. Then after a moment, when there seemed to be no danger, the animal resumed chewing.
—Michael Crichton, Jurassic Park

Imagine you are strolling leisurely in an open meadow, and a shadow suddenly moves in the periphery of your vision. How do you respond? Instinctively, your previous motions stop. You may crouch slightly in a flexed posture, and your heart rate will change as your autonomic nervous system is activated. After this momentary "arrest" response, your eyes open wide. Without willing it, your head turns in the direction of the shadow in an attempt to locate and identify it. Sense your muscles. What are they doing?

Your neck, back, legs, and feet muscles are working together to turn your body, which is now instinctively extending and lengthening. Your eyes narrow as your pelvis and head shift horizontally to give an optimal, panoramic view of your surroundings. What is your internal state? What other intangible aspects of yourself do you feel or sense in response to seeing the shadow? Most people will feel alert and engaged, curious about what it may be. Perhaps there is a hint of excitement and anticipation whetting your desire to find out what the shadow is. There may also be a sense of possible danger.

When an animal senses a change in its environment, it responds by looking for the source of the disturbance. The search may consist only of a single eye slowly scanning its surroundings. The animal orients itself toward a potential mate or source of food, and away from danger. If the change is not indicative of danger, food, or a potential mate, an animal such as the hadosaur will simply resume its previous activity. The behavior of an animal when it experiences and responds to novelty in its environment is called an "orienting response."

These instinctive responses are as primitive as the reptilian brain that organizes them. They allow an animal to respond fluidly to an ever-changing environment. All animals (including humans) possess these coordinated patterns of muscle movement and perceptual awareness. Despite our differences from the lizard and the impala, new sounds, smells, and movements in the surroundings evoke the same basic response patterns in us.

Ivan Pavlov, the great Russian physiologist, recognized and described these orienting responses in his monumental work on animal conditioning. He called the innate characteristic of this response the *"shto eta takoe"* reflex. Attempts at a literal translation have resulted in its being called the "what is it?" reflex. A more exact translation, however, suggests something closer to "what is that" or "what is going on here" or "Hey man, what's happening!", which emphasizes the amazement and curiosity inherent in the response. This dual response (reacting plus inquiring) is widely recognized as the dominant feature of orienting behaviors. For humans as well as other animals, expectancy, surprise, alertness, curiosity, and the ability to sense danger are all forms of kinesthetic and perceptual awareness that arise out of these orientation complexes. In the traumatized person, these resources are diminished. Often, any stimulus will activate the frozen (trauma) response rather than the appropriate orienting response (i.e., upon hearing a car backfire, a traumatized vet may collapse in fear).

Orienting responses are the primary means through which the animal tunes into its environment. These responses are constantly merging into one another and adapting to allow for a range of reactions and choices. The process of determining where it is, what it is, and whether it is dangerous or desirable happens first in the subconscious.

A friend recently told me a story that vividly illustrates this animal instinct in action. On a trip through Africa, Anita, her husband, and their three-year-old son went on a safari in Kenya. They were traveling through the Masai Mara desert in a van and had stopped to rest. She and her husband sat opposite one another in the car; their three-year-old son sat in her husband's lap next to an open window. They were talking about some of the animals they had seen when my friend suddenly found her body hurling across the van to slam the window shut for no apparent reason. *Then* she saw—that is, became consciously aware of the snake rising out of the grass outside the van, a few feet from her son's face.

The mother's response preceded her conscious awareness of the snake. A delay could have had deadly consequences. The instinctive brain will often orient, organize, and respond to the stimuli well before we are consciously aware of them.

Flee, Fight... or Freeze

As Grant watched, a single forearm reached up very
slowly to part the ferns beside the animals face. The limb,
Grant saw, was strongly muscled. The hand had three
grasping fingers, each ending in curved claws. The hand
gently, slowly, pushed aside the ferns. Grant felt a chill
and thought, He's hunting us. For a mammal like man,
there is something indescribably alien about the way
reptiles hunted their prey. No wonder men hated reptiles.
The stillness, the coolness, the pace was all wrong. To be
among alligators or the larger reptiles was to be remind-
ed of a different kind of life, a different kind of world...
—Michael Crichton, *Jurassic Park*

Certain species have developed mechanisms that are
especially well suited to keeping them safe. To avoid
detection and attack the zebra uses camouflage; the tur-
tle hides; moles burrow; dogs, wolves, and coyotes roll
over in a submissive posture. The behaviors of fighting,
fleeing, and freezing are so primitive that they predate
even the reptilian brain. These survival tools are found
in all species, from spiders and cockroaches to primates
and human beings.

Universal and primitive defensive behaviors are
called the "fight or flight" strategies. If the situation calls
for aggression, a threatened creature will fight. If the
threatened animal is likely to lose the fight, it will run if
it can. These choices aren't thought out; they are instinc-
tually orchestrated by the reptilian and limbic brains.
When neither fight nor flight will ensure the animal's
safety, there is another line of defense: immobility (freezing), which is just as universal and basic to survival. For
inexplicable reasons, this defense strategy is rarely given
equal billing in texts on biology and psychology. Yet, it is
an equally viable survival strategy in threatening situations. In many situations, it is the best choice.

On the biological level, success doesn't mean winning, it means surviving, and it doesn't really matter how you get there. The object is to stay alive until the danger is past and deal with the consequences later. Nature places no value judgment about which is the superior strategy. If the coyote leaves the seemingly dead opossum alone, it will recover from its immobility and walk off unconcerned about whether it could have responded in a better way. Animals do not view freezing as a sign of inadequacy or weakness, nor should we.

The purpose of running or fighting to escape danger is obvious. The efficacy of the immobility response is less apparent, yet it is equally important as a survival mechanism. Ultimately, only nature determines which instinctual responses will enhance the overall likelihood of survival for a species. No animal, not even the human, has conscious control over whether or not it freezes in response to threat. When an animal perceives that it is trapped and can't escape by running or fighting, freezing offers several advantages.

First, many predatory animals will not kill and eat an immobile animal unless they are very hungry. Immobility is an imitation of death that misleads the predator into sensing that the meat may be bad. Through this deceptive act, the prey animal has a chance to escape.

Second, predatory animals have greater difficulty detecting potential prey that are not moving. This is especially true when the prey animals coloring or appearance serves as camouflage. Some animals can only register their prey when its moving. The frog or lizard, for example, cannot detect an insect in the grass until the insect moves. In addition, many predators are not stimulated to attack a motionless prey; an inert body often doesn't evoke aggression.

Third, if a predator comes upon a group of prey animals, the collapse of an individual can distract the predator momentarily, allowing the rest of the herd to escape.

Fourth, in a world where all animals are located somewhere in the food chain and may be either predator or prey, nature provides an analgesic mechanism for minimizing the pain suffered at death.

The Return to Normal Activity

I have emphasized the immobility or freezing response because it often leads to human trauma. Animals generally suffer no such consequence from "playing" whatever their version of "possum" is. If we observe them carefully we can see how they accomplish this.

A herd of deer grazes in a forest clearing. A twig snaps. Instantly, the deer are alert—ready to flee into the forest. If cornered they may fight. Each animal becomes still. Muscles tensed, they listen and sniff the air (orientation), attempting to pinpoint the source of the sound. Deeming it insignificant, they return to leisurely chewing on their afternoon repast, cleaning and nurturing their young, and warming themselves in the morning sun. Another stimulus sends the animals back into the state of alertness and extreme vigilance (hypervigilance), once again ready to flee or fight. Seconds later, having found no actual threat, the deer again resume their former activity.

By watching the deer carefully through binoculars, one can witness the transition from the state of activated vigilance to one of normal, relaxed activity. When the animals determine that they are not in danger, they often begin to vibrate, twitch, and lightly tremble. This process begins with a very slight twitching or vibration in the upper part of the neck around the ears and spreads down into the chest, shoulders, and then finally down into the abdomen, pelvis, and hind legs. These little tremblings of muscular tissue are the organism's way of regulating extremely different states of nervous system activation. The deer move through this rhythmic cycle dozens, perhaps hundreds of times a day. This cycle occurs each time they are activated. The animals move easily and rhythmically between states of relaxed alertness and tensed hypervigilance.

Animals as Teachers

Animals in the wild provide us with a standard for health and vigor, as well as give us insight into the biological healing process. They offer us a precious glimpse of how we might function if our responses were purely instinctual. Animals are our teachers, exemplifying nature in balance.

One of the difficulties in treating trauma has been the undue focus on the content of an event that has engendered trauma. Trauma sufferers tend to identify themselves as survivors, rather than as animals with an instinctual power to heal. The animal's ability to rebound from threat can serve as a model for humans. It gives us a direction that may point the way to our own innate healing abilities. We must pay attention to our animal nature to find the instinctive strategies needed to release us from trauma's debilitating effects.

8

How Biology Becomes Pathology: Freezing

The Stage is Set

Trauma symptoms form in a spiraling process that begins with primitive biological mechanisms. At the core of this process is the immobility or freezing response, a defense mechanism summoned by the reptilian brain.

In response to threat, the organism can fight, flee, or freeze. These responses exist as parts of a unified defense system. When fight and flight responses are thwarted, the organism instinctively constricts as it moves toward its last option, the freezing response. As it constricts, the energy that would have been discharged by executing the fight or flight strategies is amplified and bound up in the nervous system. In this emotional and anxious state, the now-frustrated fight response erupts into rage; the frustrated flight response gives way to helplessness. The individual who has moved into the stage characterized by rage or helplessness still has the potential to move abruptly back into a frantic flight response or a raging counter-attack. If the organism is able to discharge the energy by fleeing or defending itself and thus resolve the threat, trauma will not occur.

Another possible scenario is that constriction will continue until the rage, terror, and helplessness have built up to a level of activation that overwhelms the nervous system. At this point, immobility will take over and the individual will either freeze or collapse. What happens then is that the intense, frozen energy, instead of discharging, gets bound up with the overwhelming, highly activated, emotional states of terror, rage, and helplessness.

Blame It on the Neo-cortex

Why don't humans just move into and out of these different responses as naturally as animals do? One reason is that our highly evolved neo-cortex (rational brain) is so complex and powerful that through fear and over-control it can interfere with the subtle restorative instinctual impulses and responses generated by the reptilian core. In particular, the neo-cortex easily overrides some of our gentler instinctual responses—such as those that guide the healing of trauma through the discharge of energy. If the discharge process is to serve its purpose, it must be initiated and driven by impulses from the reptilian brain. The neo-cortex must elaborate on instinctual information, not control it.

The neo-cortex is not powerful enough to override the instinctual defense response to threat and danger— the fight, flee, or freeze responses. In this respect, we humans are still inextricably bound to our animal heritage. Animals, however, do not have a highly evolved neo-cortex to interfere with the natural return to normal functioning through some form of discharge. In humans, trauma occurs as a result of the initiation of an instinctual cycle that is not allowed to finish. When the neo-cortex overrides the instinctual responses that would initiate the completion of this cycle, we will be traumatized.

Fear and Immobility

The duration of the immobility response in animals is normally time-limited; they go in and they come out. The human immobility response does not easily resolve itself because the supercharged energy locked in the nervous system is imprisoned by the emotions of fear and terror. The result is that a vicious cycle of fear and immobility takes over, preventing the response from completing naturally. When not allowed to complete, these responses form the symptoms of trauma. Just as terror and rage figured in the onset of the freezing response, they will now contribute greatly to its maintenance—even though there is no longer any actual threat present.

When a pigeon is quietly approached from behind (perhaps as it pecks on some grains) and is picked up gently, the bird freezes. If it is turned upside down, it will remain frozen in that position with its feet in the air for several minutes. When it comes out of this trance-like state, it will right itself and hop or fly away as though nothing had happened. However, if the pigeon is first frightened by an approaching person, it will struggle to escape. If it is caught after a frantic pursuit and held down forcibly, it will also succumb to immobility—but the terrified bird will remain frozen much longer than in the first scenario. When it comes out of its trance, it will be in a state of frantic excitability. It may thrash about wildly, pecking at almost any possible target, or fly away in a frenzy of uncoordinated movement. Fear greatly enhances and extends (i.e., potentiates) immobility. It also makes the mobilization process a fearful event.

"As They Go In, So They Come Out"

If we are highly activated and terrified upon entering the immobility state, we will move out of it in a similar manner. "As they go in, so they come out" is an expression that Army M.A.S.H. medics use when speaking of injured soldiers. If a soldier goes into surgery feeling terror and panic, he may abruptly come out of anesthesia in a state of frantic disorientation. Biologically, he is reacting like the animal fighting for its life after it has been frightened and captured. The impulse to attack in frantic rage, or to attempt a frantic escape is biologically appropriate. When captured prey come out of immobility, their survival may depend on violent aggression if the predator is still present.

Similarly, when women who have been raped begin to come out of shock (frequently, months or even years later), they often have the impulse to kill their assailants. In some instances, they may have the opportunity to carry this action through. Some of these women have been tried and sentenced for "pre-meditated" murder because the time lapse was viewed as premeditation. Some injustices may have occurred due to the misunderstanding of the biological drama that was perhaps being played out. It is possible that a number of these women may have been acting upon the profound (and delayed) self-protective responses of rage and counter-attack that they experienced coming out of agitated immobility. These reprisals may be biologically motivated, and not necessarily by premeditated revenge. Some of these killings could have been prevented by effective treatment of post-traumatic shock.

In post-traumatic anxiety, immobility is maintained primarily from within. The impulse towards intense aggression is so frightening that the traumatized person often turns it inward on themselves rather than allow it external expression. This imploded anger takes the form of anxious depression and the varied symptoms of post-traumatic stress. Like the pigeon that tries frantically to escape, but is recaptured and held prisoner once more, trauma victims beginning to exit immobility are often trapped by their own fear of abrupt activation and their potential for violence. They remain in a vicious cycle of terror, rage, and immobility. They are primed for full-out escape or raging counter-attack, but remain inhibited because of fear of violence to themselves and others.

Like Death Itself

In Chapter Seven, we discussed the biological advantage of the immobility response for prey animals. Deceiving a predator into believing its quarry is already dead often works. However, the predator is not the only actor on the stage who responds to immobility as though its prey were dead. The physiology of the immobilized animal acts as though it were dead. Animals can actually die from "immobility response overdose." The reptilian brain has ultimate control over life and death. If it receives repeated messages that the animal is dead, it may comply. In most cases, however, the reptilian brain does not constantly register that the animal is dead; therefore, there are no serious consequences. The animal remains in the immobility state for a period of time and then moves out of it through trembling discharge. The incident is completed.

Due to our highly developed brains, the process of leaving the immobility state becomes more complicated for humans. The fear of experiencing terror, rage, and violence toward oneself or others, or of being over-whelmed by the energy discharged in the mobilization process, keeps the human immobility response in place. These are not the only components that keep the freezing response from completion. The fear of death is another. Our neo-cortex informs us that immobility feels like death. Death is an experience that humans vehe-mently avoid. Animals have no such prohibitive aware-ness; for them life and death are parts of one system, a purely biological matter. Humans understand what death means and we fear it. We avoid death even in our dreams. Have you dreamt you were falling and awak-ened just before you hit the ground (or water, etc.)? Have you dreamt of being chased by someone (or thing) that is intent on harming you, only to awaken a split second before the fatal blow (stab, shot, etc.)? The fact that the immobility response feels like death is yet another rea-son the human is unable to stay with the felt sense of it long enough for it to reach its natural conclusion. Humans fear it and avoid completing it. Because most of us have a low tolerance both for going into and coming out of immobility, trauma symptoms are accumulated, maintained, and grow more complex.

If we allow ourselves to experience the death-like sensation of being frozen, and at the same time, uncou-ple the fear that accompanies it, we would be able to move through immobility. Unfortunately, these are not experiences that yield to a "grit your teeth and bear it" approach. The organism takes its cues regarding danger from its internal experience as readily as its external one. As the freezing response develops into terror, rage, or a death experience, we respond emotionally, just as we did when the event happened. The way out of im-mobility is to experience it gradually, in relative safety, through the felt sense. Remember, though it may seem interminably long, the time it takes to move through immobility is relatively short.

It's a Cumulative Effect

Post-traumatic symptoms don't develop overnight. It takes months for the freezing reaction to become symptomatic and chronic. If we know what to do, we have ample time to resolve the unfinished physiological portions of our reactions to an overwhelming event before they become entrenched as symptoms. Most of us either do not know what to do, or may not even realize that there is anything to be done. Many people walk away from overwhelming events carrying a large, unpalatable portion of unresolved trauma with them.

On the physiological level, each successive experience of freezing and re-freezing is identical to the original experience; but with one important difference. With each episode of freezing, the amount of energy summoned to deal with the situation increases due to the cumulative effects of re-freezing. The new energy necessitates the formation of more symptoms. The immobility response not only becomes chronic, it intensifies. As the frozen energy accumulates, so do the symptoms that are trying desperately to contain it.

How Biology Becomes Pathology

If large areas of our neo-cortex were destroyed, either surgically or by accident, we could still function. However, one tiny "nick" in the reptilian brain or any of its associated structures, and animal or human behavior patterns are profoundly altered. Extreme imbalance will be reflected in changed patterns of sleep, activity, aggression, eating, and sexuality. Laboratory experiments show that some animals become completely immobile, or alternatively, excessively hyperactive. They may over- or undereat to the point of death, or they will not voluntarily drink water. They may become so obsessed with sex that they are unable to attend to their other needs, or the opposite, so disinterested in sex that they will not mate and reproduce. The changes that occur are so grossly maladaptive that the animal cannot survive under ordinary conditions. These kinds of maladaptions can also be produced by electrically stimulating primitive portions of the brain. They are produced as well (though not necessarily to the same degree) by post-traumatic stress.

Regarding trauma, pathology can be thought of as the maladaptive use of any activity (physiological, behavioral, emotional, or mental) designed to help the nervous system regulate its activated energy. Pathology (i.e., symptoms) becomes, in a sense, the organism's safety valve. This valve lets off just enough pressure to keep the system running. In addition to its survival function and pain-killing effect, the immobility response is also a key part of the nervous system's circuit breaker. Without it, a human might not survive the intense activation of a serious inescapable situation without risking energetic overload. Indeed, even the symptoms that develop out of the freezing response can be viewed with a sense of appreciation and even gratitude if you consider what might happen if the system did not have this safety valve. In pathology, the organism will enlist the felt sense to experience any thought, feeling, or behavior that it can use in its effort to contain the undischarged energy mobilized for survival. The functions (such as eating, sleeping, sex, and general activity) regulated by the reptilian brain make a broad and fertile place for symptoms to take root. Anorexia, insomnia, promiscuity, and manic hyperactivity are only a few of the symptoms that can ensue when the organism's natural functions become maladaptive.

...energy is pure delight.
—William Blake

9

How Pathology Becomes Biology: Thawing

The volcanic energy of trauma discussed in Chapter Eight is bound in the coupling of fear and immobility. The key to moving through trauma is in uncoupling the immobility (which is normally time-limited) from the fear associated with it. When a frightened animal comes out of immobility, it does so with an intense readiness for counter-attack, or in a frantic, non-directed attempt to escape. For the sake of survival, all the energy that was being utilized in desperate fight or flight (before it collapsed or froze) re-emerges explosively as the animal comes out of immobility. As humans begin to emerge from immobility, we are seized often by sudden and overpowering surges of emotion. Because these surges are not immediately acted upon, this energy can become associated with enormous amounts of rage and terror. Fear and the fear of violence to self and others reactivates the immobility, extending it, often indefinitely, in the form of frozen terror. This is the vicious circle of trauma.

Nancy Re-examined: A First Step

When I tried to help Nancy (Chapter Two) relax, she began to come out of her long-held immobility reaction. The arousal and emotions of rage and terror that had been held in check most of her life broke through dramatically. In responding to the inner image of the attacking tiger, Nancy was able (decades later) to uncouple her frozen energy by completing an active escape response. In running from the imaginary tiger, Nancy was able to mobilize an intense, biologically appropriate response that allowed her—in the present—to discharge the heightened arousal that had been unleashed as her immobility began to release. By exchanging (in that highly aroused state) an active response for one of helplessness, Nancy exercised a physiological choice. Her organism was learning almost instantaneously that it didn't have to freeze. The core of traumatic reaction is

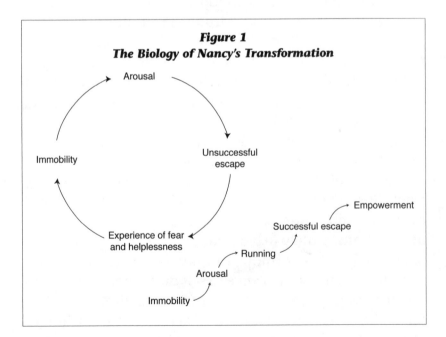

Figure 1
The Biology of Nancy's Transformation

Arousal

Immobility

Unsuccessful escape

Experience of fear and helplessness

Running

Successful escape

Empowerment

Arousal

Immobility

ultimately physiological, and it is at this level that healing begins.

It's All Energy

The forces underlying the immobility response and the traumatic emotions of terror, rage, and helplessness are ultimately biological energies. How we access and integrate this energy is what determines whether we will continue to be frozen and overwhelmed, or whether we will move through it and thaw. We have a lot going for us. Given the proper support and guidance, we can conquer our fears. With the full use of our highly developed ability to think and perceive, we can consciously move out of the trauma response. This process needs to occur gradually rather than abruptly. When working with the intensely cathartic and volatile expressions of rage, terror, and helplessness, it is best to take one small step at a time.

The drive to complete the freezing response remains active no matter how long it has been in place. When we learn how to harness it, the power of this drive becomes our greatest ally in working through the symptoms of trauma. The drive is persistent. Even if we do not do things perfectly, it will always be there to give us another chance.

Nancy's remarkable "cure" was due to the critical timing of her escape from the tiger at the very peak moment of her panic arousal. It was as though Nancy had a single chance either to escape and be cured or to tumble back into a whirlpool of overwhelming helplessness and anxiety. In the years after the session with Nancy, I began to piece together the puzzle of healing trauma. The key I found was being able to work in a gradual, gentle way with the powerful energies bound in the trauma symptoms.

Marius: A Next Step

The following description of a young man's odyssey illustrates a refinement of the strategies for healing trauma. Marius is a slight, intelligent, shy, boyish-looking
young Eskimo in his mid-twenties who was born and
raised in a remote village in Greenland. When I asked
him whether I could transcribe his session for a book,
assuring him I would disguise his name and identity, his
eyes opened wide. "No, please...It would be an honor,"
he said, "but would you please use my full name, so that
if my family and friends from my village read your book,
they will know it is me you are talking about." So this is
Marius Inuusuttoq Kristensen's story.

As a participant in a training class in Copenhagen,
Denmark, Marius reports his tendency towards anxiety
and panic, particularly when he is with a man he ad-
mires and whose approval he wants. This anxiety is
"symptomized" in his body as a weakening of the legs
and a stabbing ache on the side of his right leg, and is
often accompanied by waves of nausea. As he conveys
this experience, his head and face feel very warm and he
becomes sweaty and flushed. In talking about these feelings, he relates the following story about an event that
occurred when he was eight.

While returning from a walk alone in the mountains, he was attacked by a pack of three wild dogs and
bitten badly on his right leg. He remembers feeling the
bite, waking up in the arms of a neighbor, and has an
image of his father coming to the door and being
annoyed with him. He feels bitter, angry, and hurt by his
father's rejection. He remembers, particularly, that his
new pants were ripped and covered with blood.
Describing this, he is visibly upset. I ask him to tell me
more about the pants. They were a surprise from his
mother that morning; she had made them of polar bear

fur especially for him. His experience switches dramatically and transparently to pleasure and pride. Feeling excited, Marius holds his arms in front of himself as though feeling the soft fur and basking in the warmth of his new pants: "These are the same kind of pants that the men of the village, the hunters, wear."

He is more excited and describes seeing them with vivid, clear detail.

He imagines feeling the pants with his hands.

"Now, Marius," I ask, "can you feel your legs inside the pants?"

"Yes, I can feel my legs, they feel very strong, like the men when they are hunting."

As images and body sensation experiences unfold, he sees an expanse of rocks. I ask him to feel his pants and then look at the rocks.

"My legs want to jump; they feel light, not tight like they usually do. They are like springs, light and strong." He reports seeing the image of a long stick that is lying by a rock and picks it up.

"What is it?" I ask.

"A spear."

He goes on, "I am following a large polar bear. I am with the men, but I will make the kill." (Very small movements can be seen in his thigh, pelvic, and trunk muscles, as he imagines jumping from rock to rock in following the trail.) "I see him now. I stop and aim my spear."

"Yes," I say, "Feel that in your whole body, feel your feet on the rocks, the strength in your legs, and the arching in your back and arms, feel all that power." (This play in "dream time" helps to stimulate his instinctual, aggressive behaviors that were thwarted when he was overwhelmed by the attacking dogs. It is helping to 'prime the pump' with predatory responses that will eventually become resources in neutralizing the immo-bility-freeze collapse which occurred at the time of the attack).

"I see the spear flying," he says. Again, small pos-tural adjustments can be seen in Marius' body; he is trembling lightly now in his legs and arms. I encourage him to feel these sensations. He reports waves of excite-ment and pleasure.

"I did it. I hit him with my spear!"

"What are the men doing now?" I ask (again hop-ing to evoke predatory impulses).

"They cut the belly open and take out the inside and then cut the fur off...to...make pants and coats. Then they will carry the meat down to the village."

"Feel your pants, Marius, with your hands on your legs." I continue to help him create a resource from the sensations in his legs. These resources can then build over time, gradually increasing the possibility of escape. (With Nancy, recall it was all or none.)

Tears form in his eyes.

"Can you do this?" I ask.

"I don't know...I'm scared."

"Feel your legs, feel your pants."

He shouts in Eskimo, dramatically, in an increasing pitch. "...Yes, I cut the belly open, there is lots of blood...I take out the insides. Now I cut the skin, I rip it off, there is glistening and shimmering. It is a beautiful fur, thick and soft. It will be very warm.

Marius' body again shakes with tremors of excite-ment, strength, and conquest. The activation/arousal is quite intense and visible throughout his body. It is approaching a level similar to that when he was attacked by the dogs.

"How do you feel, Marius?"

"I'm a little scared...I don't know if I've ever felt this

much strong feeling...I think it's okay...really I feel mostly very powerful and filled with an energy, I think I can trust this... I don't know...it's strong."

"Feel your legs, feel your feet, touch the pants with your hands."

"Yes, I feel calmer now, not so much of a rush...it's more like strength."

"Okay, yes, good. Now start walking down, back towards the village." (I am directing the newly resourced man towards the traumatic moment.)

A few minutes pass, then Marius' trunk flexes and he holds still. His heart rate accelerates, and his face reddens. "I see the dogs . . . they're coming at me."

"Feel your legs, Marius, touch the pants," I demand sharply. "Feel your legs and look. What is happening?"

"I am turning, turning away. I see the dogs. I see a pole, an electricity pole. I am turning towards it. I didn't know that I remembered this." Marius pales. "I'm getting weak."

"Feel the pants, Marius," I command, "feel the pants with your hands."

"I'm running." His color returns. "I can feel my legs...they're strong, like on the rocks." Again he pales and yells out: "Agh!...my leg, it burns like fire...I can't move, I'm trying, but I can't move...I can't...I can't move, it's numb now...my leg is numb, I can't feel it."

"Turn, Marius. Turn to the dog. Look at it."

This is the critical point. I hand Marius a roll of paper towels. If he freezes now, he could be re-traumatized. He grabs the roll and strangles it as the other group members, myself included, look on with utter amazement at his strength as he twists it and almost tears it in two.

"Now the other one, look right at it...look right in its eyes."

This time he lets out screams of rage and triumph. I have him settle with his bodily sensations for a few minutes, integrating this intensity. I then ask him again to look.

"What do you see?"

"I see them...they're all bloody and dead." (His success with killing and eviscerating the imagined polar bear has prepared him for this.)

His head and eyes begin slowly turning to the right.

"What do you see?"

"I see the pole...there are bolts in it."

"Okay, feel your legs, feel your pants."

I am about to tell him to run in order to complete the running-escape response. But before I do he exclaims, "I am running...I can feel my legs, they're strong like springs." Rhythmic undulations are now visible through his pants as his entire body trembles and vibrates.

"I'm climbing...climbing...I see them below... they're dead and I'm safe." He starts to sob softly and we wait a few minutes.

"What do you experience now?"

"It feels like I'm being carried by big arms; the man has me in his arms, his hands are around mine. He's carrying me in his arms. I feel safe." Marius reports a series of images of fences and houses in the village. (He sobs softly.)

"He's knocking at the door of my family's house. The door opens...my father...he's very upset, he runs to get a towel...my leg is bleeding badly...my pants are torn...he's very upset...he's not mad at me, he's very worried. It hurts, the soap hurts." Marius sobs now in full, gentle waves. "It hurts. But I'm crying 'cause he's not angry at me...I can see he was upset and scared. I feel vibration and tingling all over, it's even and warm.

He loves me."

As Marius continues to tremble softly, his body breaks out in moist, warm beads of sweat, and I ask him, "How does it feel in your body now that your father loves you?" There is a silence.

"I feel warm, very warm and peaceful. I don't need to cry now, I'm okay and he was just scared. It's not that he doesn't love me."

Renegotiation

Initially the only image or memory of the event Marius had was the bloody pants, torn flesh, and his father's rejection. Yet here also was the positive seed of an emerging healing nucleus, his fur pants. The pants became the thread that held together the successful "renegotiaton" of the traumatic event.

The image of the ripped and bloodied pants was arousing to Marius, and his happiness was also aroused in imagining the gift of the fur pants. He was joyful when presented with this first symbol of manhood. The walk into the mountains was an initiation, a rite of passage. His pants were power objects on this "walkabout." In wanting to "jump for joy" early in the session, Marius activated resources in the form of motor patterns that were essential in eventually thawing his freezing response.

Successful renegotiation of trauma occurs when the adaptive resources of the person increase simultaneously with the arousal. In moving from the periphery of the experience to the freezing "shock core", his unresolved freezing patterns were neutralized by flexible and resolvable patterns as the activation increased.

As I encouraged Marius to gradually track the initial, positive experience with his pants towards the traumatic, freezing, "shock core", a joyful experience became linked to his earlier experience of defeat and rejection. This gave him new resources—natural aggression and competence. Armed with this newly found confidence, when Marius saw the image of the rocks, his resources began to constellate. In jumping from rock to rock and finding and picking up the stick, Marius' creative process developed these resources to propel his forward movement toward meeting the impending challenge. In being the aggressor, like the hunters, he tracked the imagined polar bear while I tracked his bodily responses. Marius had become resourced by the images and feelings of his empowered legs and the connection with the men from his village. It is with this sense of power that he sights his dangerous prey and makes the kill. Finally, approaching ecstasy, he eviscerates the imagined bear. It is of the utmost importance to understand that, even though this experience was imagined, because of the presence of the felt sense, the experience was in every way as real for Marius' as the original one, that is, mentally, physiologically, and spiritually.

In the next sequence of events, the true test is made. Empowered and triumphant, he heads back down toward the village. His awareness has expanded. For the first time, he sees and describes the road and the dogs. Previously, these images were not available to him; they were constricted in a form of amnesia. He notices that he's orienting his movements away from the attacking dogs and towards the electric pole. After experiencing the strength in his legs, Marius is no longer a prisoner of the immobility response. He now has a choice. The ecstatic trembling energy from the kill is transformed into the ability to run. This is just the beginning; he can run but cannot yet escape! I ask him to turn and face his attackers so he doesn't fall back into immobility. This time he counter-attacks, at first with rage and then with the same triumph that he experienced in the previous sequence of killing and eviscerating the bear. The plan has succeeded. Marius is now victorious and no longer a victim of defeat.

However, the renegotiation is still incomplete. In the next sequence, Marius orients himself toward the telephone pole and prepares to run. He had initiated this action years ago, but until this moment, he has not been able to execute it. With his new resources, he completes the escape by running away. This may not make sense in terms of linear time, because he has already killed his attackers. However, the sequence is completely logical to his instincts. He has now completed the immobility response that has been frozen in time since he was eight years old. A year later, I returned to Denmark and learned that Marius no longer suffered from the type of anxiety we had worked on. His renegotiation had resulted in lasting changes.

Somatic Experiencing®—*Gradated Renegotiation*

There are a number of elements in this step-wise and "mythical" renegotiation of Marius' childhood trauma. More than a thousand sessions have taught me that Marius' experience was mythically rich not because he is aboriginal, but because it is universally true that the renegotiation of trauma is an inherently mythic-poetic-heroic journey. It is a journey that belongs to all of us because we are human animals—even those of us who have never set foot outside of a city. The process of resolving trauma can move us beyond our social and cultural confinements toward a greater sense of universality. In contrast to Nancy's sudden escape from the imaginary tiger, Marius' renegotiation happened more gradually.

Somatic Experiencing is a gentle step-by-step approach to the renegotiation of trauma. The felt sense is the vehicle used to contact and gradually mobilize the powerful forces bound in traumatic symptoms. It is akin to slowly peeling the layers of skin off an onion, carefully revealing the traumatized inner core. A technical understanding of the development of these principles is beyond the scope of this book.

It is important to realize that healing trauma takes time. There may be dramatic and poignant moments as well as gradual and often mundane stretches on the road to recovery. Though Marius' healing was full of myth and drama, the key to resolving his trauma was in acknowledging and regaining his heritage as a competent, resourceful human being.

Marius' healing journey is certainly an inspiration to us all. We need to keep in mind that the germ of his healing was in the physiological discharge of the vast energy that had been bound in immobility. With Marius, we were able to find a way together to access and utilize that compressed energy in gradual steps.

For each of us, the mastery of trauma is a heroic journey that will have moments of creative brilliance, profound learning, and periods of hard tedious work. It is the process of finding ourselves a safe and gentle way of coming out of immobility without being overwhelmed. Parts of it may occur in a condensed event such as Marius' single session. Others are more open-ended, occurring gradually over time.

Elements of Renegotiation

In tracing through Marius' story we can identify elements essential to healing the effects of trauma. When Marius first begins to tell his story, he becomes riveted on his bloodied, torn pants and his father's rejection. At that moment, this single fixed image holds the meaning of the entire incident. The condensation of an entire event into a single image is characteristic of trauma. From this event, Marius was left feeling defeated, bitterly hurt, and rejected. During the session, when he feels the emotions that he has attached to the image of his bloody torn pants without trying to analyze or control them, he begins to experience a change in those feelings. Rather than defeat, hurt and rejection, his fur pants become a catalyst for grounding that inspires opposing feelings. In the image of the gift from his mother is the feeling of wanting to jump up and down with joy.

Marius, through contact with his felt sense, was able to find a rough gem in the midst of his pain and hurt. Rather than plunging into his pain, he took that jewel and began to complete, as an adult, his childhood "Walkabout" into manhood and individuation. As he joyfully receives the gift of the pants, he is able to begin to differentiate excitement from anxiety. In uncoupling the excitement and joy of living from fear, another important step is taken in waking the tiger.

In the next sequence, Marius is able to expand and deepen this excitement. By feeling the pants with his hands and feeling his legs inside the pants, Marius is beginning to establish a deep resource through the felt sense. It is through this connection with our felt sense that we are guided on our individual paths towards transformation.

In love we are swept off our feet; in trauma our legs are knocked out from under us. By re-establishing a connection with his legs as he identified with the hunters in the village, Marius became grounded in his own body and with his social world. Regaining our ground is an important step in healing trauma.

By seeing himself walking in the mountains and jumping on the rocks, Marius developed a felt sense of strength and resiliency. This resiliency is the literal springiness in our legs. It is also the resilience, metaphorically, that helps us to rebound from trauma and to move through it.

Next, as Marius tracks the imagined bear and prepares to make the kill, he mobilizes the aggression that he lost when he was overwhelmed as a child. The restoration of aggression is another key feature in healing the effects of trauma. In regaining it, Marius is empowered to take the final steps in resolving this trauma. With this newly discovered aggression, Marius transforms the complex emotion of anxiety to joy and triumphant mastery. In his imagined spearing of the bear, he makes the active response that will ensure his victory; he is no longer the vanquished child. In being able, step by step, to exchange an active, aggressive response for one of being helpless and frozen, Marius renegotiates his trauma.

At this point in the renegotiation, we see the establishment of an active escape (running) response in addition to an aggressive counter-attack response. In experiencing himself climbing the telephone pole and looking around, Marius finishes the renegotiation by completing the orienting response. This act allows him to uncouple additional fear from the excitement of being fully alive. Renegotiation helps to restore those resources that were diminished in the wake of trauma. The overall strategy of renegotiation is as follows: the first step is to develop a facility with the felt sense. Once this is developed, we can surrender to the currents of our feelings, which include trembling and other spontaneous discharges of energy. We can use the felt sense to uncouple the maladaptive attachment between excitement and fear. Because excitement is charged and we want to maintain that charge as free and distinct from anxiety, we must also be able to ground it. Resilient strength is the opposite of helplessness. The tree is made strong and resilient by its grounded root system. These roots take nourishment from the ground and grow strong. *Grounding* also allows the tree to be resilient so that it can yield to the winds of change and not be uprooted. *Springiness* is the facility to ground and "unground" in a rhythmical way. This buoyancy is a dynamic form of grounding. Aggressiveness is the biological ability to be vigorous and energetic, especially when using instinct and force. In the immobility (traumatized) state, these assertive energies are inaccessible. The restoration of healthy aggression is an essential part in the recovery from trauma. Empowerment is the acceptance of personal authority. It derives from the capacity to choose the direction and execution of one's own energies. Mastery is the possession of skillful techniques in dealing successfully with threat. Orientation is the process of ascertaining one's position relative to both circumstance and environment. In these ways the residue of trauma is renegotiated.

Because every injury exists within life and life is constantly renewing itself, within every injury is the seed of healing and renewal. At the moment our skin is cut or punctured by a foreign object, a magnificent and precise series of biochemical events is orchestrated through evolutionary wisdom. The body has been designed to renew itself through continuous self-correction. These same principles also apply to the healing of psyche, spirit, and soul.

II
Symptoms of Trauma

10

The Core of the Traumatic Reaction

Arousal—What Goes Up Must Come Down

When we perceive danger or sense that we are threatened, we become aroused. Arousal is the activity that energizes our survival responses. Imagine you are standing at the edge of a steep cliff. As you look down, observe the jagged rocks below. Now, notice what you are experiencing in your body. In this situation, most people will become aroused in some way. Many of us will experience a rush of energy which may be felt as a flash of heat or an increased heart rate. You may notice a tightening of throat and anal sphincter muscles. Others may feel exhilarated by the close proximity to danger and find it challenging.

Most of us enjoy the "natural high" we get from wild arousal. Many of us seek out "near-death" experiences like bungee-jumping, skydiving, and paragliding because of the euphoric feeling that comes with extreme states of arousal. I have worked and talked with numerous war veterans who lament the fact that they have not felt fully alive since they were in the "heat of battle." Human beings long to be challenged by life, and we need the arousal that energizes us to meet and overcome these challenges. Deep satisfaction is one of the fruits of a completed arousal cycle. The cycle looks like this: we are challenged or threatened, then aroused; the arousal peaks as we mobilize to face the challenge or threat; then, the arousal is actively brought down, leaving us relaxed and satisfied.

Traumatized people have a deep distrust of the arousal cycle, usually for good reason. This is because to a trauma victim, arousal has become coupled with the overwhelming experience of being immobilized by fear. Because of this fear, the traumatized person will prevent or avoid completion of the arousal cycle, and remain stuck in a cycle of fear. The key for trauma victims is becoming reacquainted with a simple natural law. What goes up must come down. When we can trust the arousal cycle and are able to flow with it, the healing of trauma will begin.

Following are some of the most common signs of arousal:

- physical—increase in heart rate, difficulty breathing (rapid, shallow, panting, etc.), cold sweats, tingling muscular tension
- mental—increase in thoughts, mind racing, worrying

If we allow ourselves to acknowledge these thoughts and sensations using the felt sense and let them have their natural flow, they will peak, then begin to diminish and resolve. As this process occurs, we may experience trembling, shaking, vibration, waves of warmth, fullness of breath, slowed heart rate, warm sweating, relaxation of the muscles, and an overall feeling of relief, comfort and safety.

Trauma Is Trauma, No Matter What Caused It

Trauma occurs when an event creates an unresolved

impact on an organism. Resolution is accomplished through working with this unresolved impact through the felt sense. Reliving the event in itself may seem valuable, but too often it is not. Traumatic symptoms sometimes mimic or recreate the event that caused them; however, healing requires an ability to get in touch with the process of the traumatic response.

The following exercise will help you understand why the organism's response to a threatening event is more important than the event that caused it. The exercise doesn't deal with trauma itself, but with the physiological response that initiates the potential for trauma. The exercise will also help clarify what trauma feels like (which is similar from person to person), and tells how to identify it.

Exercise

If you feel overwhelmed or deeply disturbed during any part of this exercise, please stop. The exercise may be too activating for some people. If this is true for you, I suggest you seek qualified professional help.

For this exercise you will need a pencil, paper, and a clock or watch with a second hand or a digital display. (If you don't have such a timepiece, you can do the exercise without it.) With pencil in hand and the clock or watch where you can see it, find a comfortable position and contact your felt sense. Tune into your arms and legs, and feel the sensation of your body being supported by whatever you are sitting on; now add to your awareness any other sensations that are present—the feeling of your clothes on your skin, the weight of the book in your lap, etc. You will need this awareness to do the exercise.

Once you have a sense of how your body feels on the level of sensation, continue when you are comfortable. Proceed step by step through the exercise. For the best results do the entire exercise in one sitting. Read through it before you do it. As you read and experience it, get in touch with your feelings and thoughts through the felt sense.

Part One: Sit comfortably and pretend you are in an air-plane flying at 30,000 feet across the country. There has been some turbulence, but nothing out of the ordinary. Keep your awareness engaged as fully as possible and tune into your felt sense. Imagine that you suddenly hear a loud explosion—BOOM—followed by complete silence. The plane's engines have stopped. How does your body respond?

Notice the response in your breathing—
In your heartbeat—
The temperature in different parts of your body—
In vibrations and involuntary twitching and the intensity of movements—
In your overall posture—
In your eyes—
In your neck—
In your sight and hearing—
In your muscles—
In your abdomen—
In your legs—
For each item, make a short note of your responses.
Make a note of the current time in minutes and seconds.
Take a deep breath and relax. Let your body return to the level of comfort you experienced before you started the exercise. Focus on the felt sense of that comfort and when you feel that you are ready to move on to the next part of the exercise. Make a note of the time in minutes and seconds.

Part Two: Visualize yourself sitting on the front step of some friends' house waiting for them to come home. It's a warm day and the sky is clear. You aren't in a hurry so it feels comfortable to just lean back and enjoy the day while you wait for your friends to arrive. Suddenly, a man you had noticed walking on the street begins running straight toward you screaming and waving a gun. How does your body respond?

Finish the exercise as you did in Part One.

Part Three: Pretend you are driving your car on the freeway. Traffic isn't bad, but your destination is still twenty minutes away. You decide this would be a good time to listen to some music. You have just reached for the radio when a semi-truck careens across the center divider and heads straight for your car. How does your body respond?

Finish the exercise as you did in the previous parts.

Part Four: Compare your answers for the first three parts of the exercise. How similar are your responses to each of the three scenarios?

What is different?

How easy is it for you to relax now?

Make a note of the time it took you to relax after each exercise.

Most people will have similar responses to all three scenarios. Any potentially traumatizing event, real or imagined, results in certain physiological responses that vary from person to person, primarily in their magnitude. This response is a generic phenomenon throughout the animal kingdom. If you personally find it difficult to control your arousal, then open your eyes and focus on some (pleasant) aspect of your environment. Whenever humans or animals lack the resources to successfully deal with a dangerous event, the arousal and other physiological changes that mark their response to the event will be essentially the same. Because everyone experiences the early stages of trauma in a similar way, you can learn to recognize this experience just as the exercise above taught you to recognize the initial response to danger. Once again, the place to look for these similarities is in the felt sense. How do they register in your body?

The Core of the Traumatic Reaction

There are four components of trauma that will always be present to some degree in any traumatized person:

1. hyperarousal
2. constriction
3. dissociation
4. freezing (immobility), associated with the feeling of helplessness.

Together, these components form the core of the traumatic reaction. They are the first to appear when a traumatic event occurs. Throughout our lives, we have all experienced these as normal responses. However, when they occur together over an extended period of time, they are an almost certain indication that we have experienced an event that has left us with unresolved traumatic residue.

When we learn to recognize these four components of the traumatic reaction, we are well on our way to recognizing trauma. All other symptoms develop from these four if the defensive energy mobilized to respond to a traumatic event is not discharged or integrated within a few days, weeks, or months following the experience.

Hyperarousal

During times of conflict or stress, most people experience symptoms such as increased heartbeat and breathing, agitation, difficulty in sleeping, tension, muscular jitteriness, racing thoughts, or perhaps an anxiety attack.

Though not always indicative of traumatic symptoms, these signs are usually due to some form of hyperarousal. If hyperarousal, constriction, dissociation, and a sense of helplessness form the core of the traumatic reaction, then hyperarousal is the seed in that core.

If you reflect back on the previous exercise, you will realize that it invoked at least a mild version of hyperarousal. Whenever this heightened internal arousal occurs, it is primarily an indication that the body is summoning its energetic resources to mobilize against a potential threat. When the situation is serious enough to threaten the organism's very survival, the amount of energy mobilized is much higher than that mobilized for any other situation in our lives. Unfortunately, even when we know that we need to discharge the aroused energy, doing so is not always easy. Like many instinctual processes, hyperarousal cannot be voluntarily controlled. The following exercise is a simple way to experientially confirm this.

Exercise

During the three scenarios you experienced in the last exercise, did you imagine or create the responses in your body or were they produced by your body as an involuntary response to the scenarios you envisioned? In other words, did you make them happen or did they happen on their own?

Now attempt to deliberately make your body have such a response without envisioning a threatening scenario. Use a direct approach and see if you can make your body produce responses similar to those you experienced in the three scenarios—

In your eyes.
In your posture.
In your muscles.

In your level of arousal.

Now try all the parts of the experience together at the same time.

When you compare your experience in this exercise to your experience in the earlier one, how is it similar? How is it different?

When attempting the exercise above, most people can duplicate the physical posture, the muscle contractions, and the movements that accompany hyperarousal to some degree, though generally not with the same level of coordination and synchronicity that accompanies the real thing. Heightened internal arousal is much more likely to happen if you do all the parts of the physical response at once rather than one at a time. Even doing them one at a time is more effective than saying, "Nervous system, become hyperaroused." The vast majority of people will not be able to mobilize the same level of arousal using this kind of direct, deliberate approach. It just doesn't work. Hyperarousal is the nervous system's response to threat, whether that threat is internal, external, real, or imagined.

In the short term, the three other components comprising the core of traumatic reaction—constriction, dissociation, and helplessness—operate to protect the organism. These natural functions protect us from the external threat that initiated the aroused response as well as from the internal threat that develops when the aroused energy is not used for active defense. Trauma symptoms begin to develop as short-term solutions to the dilemma of undischarged energy. When they do develop, the constellation of symptoms is organized around a dominant theme. Not surprisingly, these themes are constriction, dissociation, and helplessness.

Constriction

Refer to your notes for the first exercise in this chapter. How many of the body responses indicate some form of constriction, tension, or tightening?

In terms of the body, constriction is a system-wide phenomenon. It dominates our earliest experience of threat, essentially affecting every function and part of the body.

When we respond to a life-threatening situation, hyperarousal is initially accompanied by constriction in our bodies and perceptions. The nervous system acts to ensure that all our efforts can be focused on the threat in a maximally optimal way. Constriction alters a person's breathing, muscle tone, and posture. Blood vessels in the skin, extremities, and viscera constrict so that more blood is available to the muscles which are tensed and prepared to take defensive action.

Perceptual awareness of the environment also constricts so that our full attention is directed toward the threat. This is a form of hypervigilance. Hikers who suddenly see a rattlesnake coiled up on the path in front of them will not hear the babbling brook or the birds calling from the trees. They will not notice the delicate wildflowers or the intricate pattern of the lichens on a rock, nor will they be concerned about what to eat for lunch or whether they are getting too much sun. At that moment, their attention will be focused completely on the snake. We have all heard stories of people who are able to accomplish extraordinary feats of courage and strength during times of threat. The woman who is able to lift the car that has fallen on her teenage son as he changed the oil is using the energy mobilized by the nervous system to help her meet and successfully deal with this potentially life-threatening situation. Hyperarousal and constriction cooperate in enabling her to accomplish a task she could never successfully execute under normal conditions. If she were to become overwhelmed and remain inactive in the hyperaroused and constricted state, some of that unresolved energy would be channeled into continued hyperarousal. The rest would be used to maintain constriction and a myriad of similarly organized but more complex traumatic symptoms: e.g., chronic hypervigilance, anxiety or panic attacks, or intrusive imagery (flashbacks, terrifying visualizations).

When constriction fails to sufficiently focus the organism's energy to defend itself, the nervous system evokes other mechanisms such as freezing and dissociation to contain the hyperarousal. Constriction, dissociation and freezing form the full battery of responses that the nervous system uses to deal with the scenario in which we must defend ourselves, but cannot.

Dissociation

I'm not afraid of dying. I just don't want to be there when it happens.
—Woody Allen

In this characteristic one-liner, Woody Allen quips a fairly accurate description of the role played by dissociation—it protects us first from the impact of escalating arousal. If a life-threatening event continues, dissociation protects us from the pain of death. In his personal diary, the explorer David Livingstone graphically recorded this encounter with a lion on the plains of Africa:

"I heard a shout. Startled, in looking half round, I saw the lion just in the act of springing upon me. I was upon a little height; he caught my shoulder as he sprang, and we both came to the ground below together.

Growling horribly close to my ear, he shook me as a terrier does a rat. The shock produced a stupor similar to that which seems to be felt by a mouse after the first shake of the cat. *It caused a sort of dreaminess in which there was no sense of pain nor feeling of terror, though quite conscious of all that was happening. It was like what patients partially under the influence of chloroform describe, who see all the operation, but feel not the knife. This singular condition was not the result of any mental process. The shake annihilated fear, and allowed no sense of horror in looking round at the beast.* This peculiar state is probably produced in all animals killed by the carnivore; and if so, is a merciful provision by our benevolent creator for lessening the pain of death." [Italics mine]

The best way to define dissociation is through the experience of it. In its mildest forms, it manifests as a kind of spaciness. At the other end of the spectrum, it can develop into so-called multiple personality syndrome. Because dissociation is a breakdown in the continuity of a person's felt sense, it almost always includes distortions of time and perception. A mild variety of this symptom is responsible for the experience many people have when driving home from the corner store; suddenly, they find themselves arriving home with no memory of how they got there—the last thing they remember is driving away from the store. Dissociation is also operating when we put our keys down "somewhere" and then can't remember where. At such times, we may tacitly acknowledge the momentary absence of the felt sense by facetiously referring to ourselves or others as having been "spaced out," or "out to lunch." In other words, out of our bodies. These are some of the forms that dissociation takes in our everyday lives. It enters into our experience specifically when we are faced with life-threatening situations. Imagine driving your car around a sharp curve on a narrow mountain road. Suddenly, you have to swerve to avoid a head-on collision with a truck coming straight at you. As you skid toward the narrow shoulder, watch the images unfold in slow motion. Then, with a fearless calm, notice that you are viewing someone else from the sidelines instead of confronting your own death.

Similarly, the woman being raped, the soldier facing enemy fire, or the victim of an accident may experience a fundamental disconnection from his or her body. From a corner of the ceiling, a child may watch him/herself being molested, and feel sorry for or neutral toward the defenseless child below.

Dissociation is one of the most classic and subtle symptoms of trauma. It is also one of the most mysterious. The mechanism through which it occurs is less easily explained than the experience of it or the role it plays. In trauma, dissociation seems to be a favored means of enabling a person to endure experiences that are at the moment beyond endurance—like being attacked by a lion, a rapist, an oncoming car, or a surgeon's knife. Dissociation can become chronic and evolve into more complex symptoms when the hyperaroused energy is not discharged.

Individuals who have been repeatedly traumatized as young children often adopt dissociation as a preferred mode of being in the world. They dissociate readily and habitually without being aware of it. Even individuals who do not dissociate habitually will dissociate when they become aroused or when they begin to access uncomfortable traumatic images or sensations. In either case, dissociation serves a valuable role in helping to keep the undischarged energy of hyperarousal disconnected from the fullness of our experience. At the same time, dissociation interrupts the continuity of the felt sense, and in so doing, prevents traumatized people from working effectively on resolving their traumatic symptoms. The point here is not to eliminate dissociation, but to increase one's awareness of it.

Exercise

To get a sense of how dissociation feels, sit comfortably in a chair and imagine that you are lying on a raft that is floating on a lake. Feel yourself floating, then allow yourself to gently float out of your body. Float up to the sky like a slowly rising balloon and watch yourself sitting down there below.

What is the experience like?

What happens when you try to sense your body?

Move between your body and the floating feeling a few more times to get a sense of how dissociation feels.

While some people find this exercise simple to do, others will find it very difficult. As we mentioned earlier, trauma symptoms can be organized around constriction or dissociation. Not surprisingly, people who favor the dissociative symptoms find dissociative exercises easier to do than people who favor constriction. If you found the floating exercise difficult, try the one that follows—it may be easier for you.

Exercise

Sit comfortably in a chair that supports your body. Begin the exercise by thinking of a place where you would really like to take a vacation—a long, leisurely, expense-paid vacation. It's going to be a great vacation, so be sure to mentally review your geography carefully so that you pick the best spot. Now fantasize to your heart's content:

Have fun...

Enjoy...

Just before you are ready to come back, answer this

question:

Where are you?

Chances are you chose your favorite vacation spot. You are not likely to say that you are in your body. When you are not in your body, you are dissociated. Congratulations.

Do the exercise again to reinforce your ability to recognize dissociation when it happens. Remember, the point of these exercises is not to prevent dissociation from happening. The point is to be able to recognize it as it happens. It is possible to be dissociated and to simultaneously be aware of what is occurring around you. This dual consciousness is important for beginning the process of healing and re-association. If you feel resistant to learning about this dual consciousness, your organism may be sending you a signal that dissociation plays an important role in organizing your traumatic symptoms. If you do feel resistance, honor it and proceed slowly. Remind yourself from time to time that dual consciousness is possible, and occasionally attempt it.

Dissociation, as it is presented here, occurs in a variety of ways, each having a common fundamental disconnection between either the person and the body, a part of the body, or a part of the experience. It may occur as a split between:

1. the consciousness and the body.
2. one part of the body, such as the head or the limbs and the rest of the body.
3. the self and the emotions, thoughts, or sensations.
4. the self and the memory of part or all of the event.

The way dissociation occurs will influence the way that more complex symptoms develop. In addition, there seems to be evidence that the use of dissociation as a response to trauma is influenced by both genetics and personality structure.

Spaciness and forgetfulness are among the more obvious symptoms that evolve from dissociation. However, there are other symptoms that are less easily recognized as originating from it. Among these are the following:

• *Denial* is probably a lower-level energy form of dissociation. The disconnection is between the person and the memory of or feelings about a particular event (or series of events). We may deny that an event occurred, or we may act as though it were unimportant. For instance, when someone we love dies or when we are injured or violated, we may act as though nothing has happened because the emotions that come with truly acknowledging the situation are too painful. Then suddenly, we may be consumed with intense emotion. Denial gives way to fear, anger, sorrow, or shame as the feelings once again integrate and the energy that has been bound up in the denial is released. However, when the bound-up energy is too great and the feelings too painful, denial can become chronic—a "set in stone" insistence that an event never happened.

• *Physical ailments* are often the result of partial or compartmentalized dissociation where one part of the body is out of touch with other parts. A disconnection between the head and the rest of the body can produce headaches. PMS can be the result of a disconnection between organs in the pelvic region and the rest of the body. Similarly, gastrointestinal symptoms (e.g., irritable bowel syndrome), recurring back problems, and chronic pain can result from partial dissociation compounded by constriction.

Helplessness

Helplessness is closely related to the primitive, universal, biological response to overwhelming threat—the freezing response. If hyperarousal is the nervous system's accelerator, a sense of overwhelming helplessness is its brake. Those who have read *Watership Down* may remember the way the rabbits froze when they saw headlights coming at them in the dark. This is the freezing response; in the story, the rabbits called it "tharn."

Unlike the automobile in which the brake and accelerator are designed to operate at different times, with a traumatic reaction both brake and accelerator operate together. Since the nervous system only recognizes that the threat has passed when the mobilized energy has been discharged, it will keep mobilizing energy indefinitely until the discharge happens. At the same time, the nervous system recognizes that the amount of energy in the system is too much for the organism to handle and it applies a brake so powerful that the entire organism shuts down on the spot. With the organism completely immobilized, the tremendous energy in the nervous system is held in check.

The helplessness that is experienced at such times is not the ordinary sense of helplessness that can affect anyone from time to time. The sense of being completely immobilized and helpless is not a perception, belief, or a trick of the imagination. It is real. The body cannot move. This is abject helplessness—a sense of paralysis so profound that the person cannot scream, move, or feel. Of the four key components that form the core of the traumatic reaction, helplessness is the one you are least likely to have experienced, unless you have suffered an overwhelming threat to your life. Yet, this profound sense of helplessness is nearly always present in the early stages of "overwhelm" resulting from a traumatic event.

If you closely examine your reactions to the three scenarios in the exercise at the beginning of the chapter, you may be able to identify a very mild version of helplessness. When the event is real and unfolding in a truly disastrous way, the effect of helplessness is drastically amplified. Later, when the threat is over, the intense helplessness and immobilization effects will wear off, but not completely. When we are traumatized, an echo of this feeling of being frozen remains with us.

Like hyperarousal and constriction, helplessness is an overt reflection of the physiological processes happening in the body. When our nervous systems shift into an aroused state in response to danger, and we cannot defend ourselves or flee, the next strategy the nervous system employs is immobilization. Nearly every creature that lives has this primitive response wired into its repertoire of defensive strategies. We will return again and again to this intriguing response in the chapters that follow. It plays a leading role in both the development and transformation of trauma.

And Then There Was Trauma

Hyperarousal, constriction, helplessness, and dissociation are all normal responses to threat. As such, they do not always end up as traumatic symptoms. Only when they are habitual and chronic do symptoms develop. As these stress reactions remain in place, they form the groundwork and fuel for the development of subsequent symptoms. Within months, these symptoms at the core of the traumatic reaction will begin to incorporate mental and psychological characteristics into their dynamics until eventually they reach into every corner of the trauma sufferer's life.

In short, with trauma, the stakes are high. Ideally,

the exercises in this chapter combined with other experiences you have had will help you identify how these reactions feel. As they become chronic, hyperarousal, constriction, helplessness, and dissociation together produce an anxiety so intense it can become unbearable. Eventually, the symptoms can coalesce into traumatic anxiety, a state that pervades the trauma sufferer's every waking (and sleeping) moment.

The symptoms that comprise the core of the traumatic reaction are the surest way to know that trauma has occurred—if you can recognize how they feel. As the constellation of symptoms grows increasingly complex, some combination of these four components of the core of the traumatic reaction will always be present. When you can recognize them, these components will help you distinguish between symptoms that are due to trauma and those that are not.

11

Symptoms of Trauma

When our nervous systems prepare us to meet danger, they shift into highly energized states. If we can discharge this energy while actively and effectively defending against threat (or shortly after the threatening event), the nervous system will move back toward a normal level of functioning. Our felt sense will feel complete, self-satisfied, and heroic. If the threat has not been dealt with successfully, the energy stays in our bodies. We have now created a self-perpetuating dilemma. On a physiological level, our bodies and minds work in tandem as one integrated system. We know that we are in danger when we perceive an external threat and our nervous system becomes highly aroused.

The perception of an actual threat signals danger, as does the activated state (even without the perception). You get the message that you are in danger not only through what you actually see (even peripherally), but through sensations that come from the unconscious visceral experience of your physiological state. The threatening person coming toward you signals danger, but so does the fact that your body is responding with an increased heartbeat, tightened stomach muscles, a

145

heightened and constricted awareness of the immediate environment, and altered muscle tone (in general). When the energy of this highly activated state is not discharged, the organism concludes that it is still in danger. The effect of that perception on the organism is that it continues to re-stimulate the nervous system in order to maintain and augment that level of preparedness and arousal.

When this occurs the debilitating symptoms of trauma are born. The nervous system activates all its physiological and biochemical mechanisms for dealing with threat, yet it cannot sustain this heightened level of arousal without the opportunity or means to respond effectively. The nervous system alone is incapable of discharging energy. This creates a self-perpetuating cycle of activation that will overload the system if it continues indefinitely. The organism must find a way out of the cycle created by the perception of danger and the accompanying arousal in order to regain its equilibrium. Failure to do so leads to pathology and debilitation as the organism compensates for its aroused state through the manifestations that are now recognized as the symptoms of trauma.

Symptoms

The nervous system compensates for being in a state of self-perpetuating arousal by setting off a chain of adaptations that eventually bind and organize the energy into "symptoms." These adaptations function as a safety valve to the nervous system. The first symptoms of trauma usually appear shortly after the event that engendered them. Others will develop over time. As I mentioned earlier, trauma symptoms are energetic phenomena that serve the organism by providing an organized way to manage and bind the tremendous energy contained in both the original and the self-perpetuated response to threat.

Due to the uniqueness of each individual's experience, it would be a prohibitive task to compile a complete list of every known trauma symptom. However, there are symptoms that are indicators of trauma because they are common to most traumatized people. In spite of the vast diversity of possibilities available to it, the nervous system does seem to favor some symptoms over others.

Generally, some traumatic symptoms are more likely to appear sooner than others. In the last chapter we discussed the first symptoms to develop. (the core of the traumatic reaction):

- hyperarousal
- constriction
- dissociation (including denial)
- feelings of helplessness

Other early symptoms that begin to show up at the same time or shortly after those above are:

- hypervigilance (being "on guard" at all times)
- intrusive imagery or flashbacks
- extreme sensitivity to light and sound
- hyperactivity
- exaggerated emotional and startle responses
- nightmares and night terrors
- abrupt mood swings: e.g., rage reactions or temper tantrums, shame
- reduced ability to deal with stress (easily and frequently stressed out)
- difficulty sleeping

Several of the symptoms above can also show up in the next phase of development, as well as in the last. The list is not for diagnostic purposes. It is a guide to help you get a feel for how trauma symptoms behave. Symptoms that generally occur in this next stage of development include:

- panic attacks, anxiety, and phobias
- mental "blankness" or "spaciness"
- exaggerated startle response
- extreme sensitivity to light and sound
- hyperactivity
- exaggerated emotional responses
- nightmares and night terrors
- avoidance behavior (avoiding certain circumstances)
- attraction to dangerous situations
- frequent crying
- abrupt mood swings: e.g., rage reactions or temper tantrums, shame
- exaggerated or diminished sexual activity
- amnesia and forgetfulness
- inability to love, nurture, or bond with other individuals
- fear of dying, going crazy, or having a shortened life
- reduced ability to deal with stress (easily and frequently stressed out)
- difficulty with sleep

The final group of symptoms are those that generally take longer to develop. In most cases they have been preceded by some of the earlier symptoms. You may notice that some symptoms appear on all three lists. There is no fixed rule that determines which symptom the organism will choose to enlist, or when it will choose to enlist it. Remember, none of these lists are by any means complete. Symptoms that generally develop last include:

- excessive shyness
- muted or diminished emotional responses

- inability to make commitments
- chronic fatigue or very low physical energy
- immune system problems and certain endocrine problems such as thyroid dysfunction
- psychosomatic illnesses, particularly headaches, neck and back problems, asthma, digestive, spastic colon, and severe premenstrual syndrome
- depression, feelings of impending doom
- feelings of detachment, alienation, and isolation — "living dead"
- diminished interest in life
- fear of dying, going crazy, or having a shortened life
- frequent crying
- abrupt mood swings, e.g., rage reactions or temper tantrums, shame
- exaggerated or diminished sexual activity
- amnesia and forgetfulness
- feelings and behaviors of helplessness
- inability to love, nurture, or bond with other individuals
- difficulty with sleep
- reduced ability to deal with stress and to formulate plans

Obviously, not all these symptoms are caused exclusively by trauma, nor has everyone who exhibits one or more of these symptoms been traumatized. The flu, for instance, can cause malaise and abdominal discomfort that is similar to trauma symptoms. However, there is a difference; symptoms produced by the flu generally go away in a few days. Those produced by trauma do not. The symptoms of trauma can be stable (ever-present), unstable (will come and go), or they can hide for decades. Generally, these symptoms do not occur individually, but in constellations. These "syndromes" often grow increasingly complex over time, becoming less and less connected with the original trauma experience. While certain symptoms can suggest a particular type of trauma, no symptom is exclusively indicative of the trauma that caused it. People will manifest traumatic symptoms differently, depending on the nature and severity of the trauma, the situation in which it occurred, and the personal and developmental resources available to the individual at the time of the experience.

And Around and Around We Go

Relaxing makes me nervous.
—Unknown

As I have mentioned repeatedly, the perception of threat in the presence of undischarged arousal creates a self-perpetuating cycle. One of the most insidious characteristics of trauma symptoms is that they are hooked into the original cycle in such a way that they are also self-perpetuating. This characteristic is the primary reason why trauma is resistant to most forms of treatment. For some people, this self-perpetuating cycle keeps their symptoms stable. Others develop one or a variety of additional behaviors or predispositions (all of which may be considered trauma symptoms) to help the nervous system keep the situation under control.

Avoidance behaviors. Trauma symptoms are the organism's way of defending itself against the arousal generated by an ever-present perception of threat. This defense system, however, is not sophisticated enough to withstand much stress. Stress causes the system to break down, releasing the original arousal energy and its message of danger. Unfortunately, when we live with the aftereffects of trauma, simply avoiding stressful situations is not sufficient to prevent the breakdown of the defense systems. If we tiptoe around arousal, our nervous systems will create their own. When this happens, we cannot rebound from the impacts of everyday frustrations as easily as we could if our nervous systems were free to function fully and normally.

Ordinary circumstances can disturb the delicate organization of energy in the traumatized individual's nervous system. A traumatized person may develop so-called "avoidance behaviors" to help keep the underlying arousal in place. Avoidance behaviors are a form of trauma symptom in which we limit our lifestyles to situations that are not potentially activating. Fearing another near accident, we may develop a reluctance to drive. If the excitement of a ball game triggered a panic attack, ball games may suddenly be less appealing. If flashbacks occur during a sexual encounter, this may lead to a diminished interest in sex. Any event that causes a change in our usual energy levels has potential to trigger uncomfortable emotions and sensations. Gradually, our lives will become more and more constricted as we try to avoid circumstances that might cause the usual balance of energy to shift.

Fear of so-called negative emotion. When the usual balance of energy shifts, we begin to re-experience the event. Here the picture becomes more complicated because what we are experiencing is due in part to confusion about the nature of the energy that is released.

In its pure form, the energy generated by our nervous system to protect us from danger is vital. It feels alive and exhilarating. When this energy is thwarted in its attempt to protect us, a significant portion of it is re-channeled into fear, rage, hatred, and shame as part of the constellation of symptoms that develop to organize the undischarged energy. These so-called "negative" emotions become intimately associated with the vital energy itself, as well as with the other symptoms that form the cluster of traumatic aftereffects.

When we suffer from trauma, the association between the life energy and the negative emotions is so close that we cannot distinguish between them. Discharge is precisely what we need, but when it begins to happen, the effect can be terrifying and intolerable, in part because the energy released is perceived to be negative. Because of this fear, we typically suppress the energy or at best discharge it incompletely.

Drug therapy and substance abuse. Another means by which traumatized people can attempt to stabilize or suppress symptoms is through drug therapy. We often try this approach at the recommendation of a doctor, or we may attempt to self-medicate (substance abuse).

Whatever means of stabilization we employ, our purpose is to create a stable environment. This feat requires a container that is energetically strong enough that the symptoms will not be stressed or challenged. These containers are like dams. They must be engineered well enough to prevent the release of horrible fear and primitive, uncontrollable rage. Trauma sufferers often find ourselves on a treadmill over which we have no control. We may be driven to avoid situations that evoke both authentic excitement and relaxation, because either could disrupt the equilibrium that our symptoms need to maintain their stability.

Out of the Loop

There are ways out of these self-perpetuating cycles. Somatic Experiencing® is one of them. In learning to define trauma by its symptoms, rather than by the event that caused it, we can develop perspectives that will help us recognize trauma when it occurs. This will enable us to flow with our natural responses rather than blocking the innate healing process.

The journey back to health and vitality is anything but immediate. Any step, however small, is significant and noteworthy. Unlike so many of the other journeys we undertake in the course of our growth and development, this journey has a finish—a resolution that leaves us richer and fuller for having accomplished it. Life is difficult enough when we are healthy and vital. When we are fragmented by trauma, it can be unbearable. As you will see in later chapters, each small step toward wholeness becomes a resource that can be used to enhance and support the healing that will unfold when we align with our natural selves.

There is a way to take back the control of our bodies that is lost when traumatic aftereffects become chronic. It is possible to deliberately stimulate the nervous system into becoming aroused and then to gently discharge the arousal. Remember, hyperarousal and its allied mechanisms are a direct result of the energy involuntarily mobilized by the nervous system specifically in response to threat. These mechanisms originate in the nervous system; you experience them in your body. It is in your body—with the nervous system fully engaged and accessed through the felt sense—that you will be successful in working with them.

12

A Traumatized Person's Reality

The premise of this book is that trauma is part of a natural physiological process that simply has not been allowed to be completed. It is not primarily a derivative of the individual's personality—at least not initially.

In Chapter Ten we discussed how the four basic symptoms of trauma—hyperarousal, constriction, dissociation, and helplessness—are directly attributable to the physiological changes that occur when we are overwhelmed while responding to a life-threatening event. In this chapter, we will track the experience of these symptoms.

The Threat That Can't Be Found

Few symptoms provide more insight into a traumatic experience than hypervigilance. Hypervigilance is a direct and immediate manifestation of hyperarousal, which is the initial response to threat. Its effect on the orienting response is particularly debilitating, setting the traumatized individual up for an ongoing experience of fear, paralysis, and victimization.

Hypervigilance occurs when the hyperarousal that

accompanies the initial response to danger activates an amplified, compulsive version of the orienting response. This distorted orienting response is so compelling that the individual feels utterly driven to identify the source of the threat even though it is a response to internal arousal rather than anything sensed in the external environment.

When arousal continues (because discharging it is too threatening), we find ourselves in a no-win situation. We feel compelled to find a source of threat, but the compulsion is internally generated and even if an external source of threat is identified, the compulsive, hypervigilant stance will continue because the internal arousal is still present. We will persistently try to find the source of the threat (where is it?) and identify it (what is it?), because that is what the primitive orienting response is programmed to do when the nervous system becomes aroused. The catch is that there is often no threat to be found.

Hypervigilance becomes one of the ways we manage the excess energy resulting from an unsuccessful defense against an original threat. We use hypervigilance to channel some of that energy into the muscles of the head, neck, and eyes in an obsessive search for danger. When combined with the internal arousal that is still present, our rational brains can become irrational. They begin to search for and identify external sources of danger. This maladaptive practice channels much of the energy into a specific activity that will become more and more repetitive and compulsive. In the hypervigilant state, all change—including changes in our own internal states—is perceived as a threat. What may appear to be unfounded paranoia may actually be our interpretation of the excitement of sexual arousal or even the effect of caffeine in a soft drink.

As the freezing response gradually becomes more and more entrenched, the tendency for hypervigilance and defense grows stronger. Hypervigilant people are keyed to a state of intense alertness at all times and may actually develop a slightly furtive or fearful, open-eyed appearance due to this constant watchfulness. There is a growing tendency to see danger where there is none, and a diminished capacity to experience curiosity, pleasure, and the joy of life. All of this occurs because, at the core of our beings, we simply do not feel safe.

Consequently, we will continually be on edge, ready to initiate a defensive response, but unable to execute it coherently. We search compulsively for the threat that can't be found, even when a real threat stands before us. The nervous system can become so activated that it cannot readily tune down. As a result, behavioral and physiological rhythms (e.g., sleep) may be disturbed. We will be unable to unwind or relax, even in those moments when we feel safe enough to do so.

Mrs. Thayer

Mrs. Thayer, a character in "The Wind Chill Factor," a short story by M.K. Fischer, provides a vivid and accurate example of how hypervigilance operates. Mrs. Thayer is a physician who is staying alone in a friend's cottage on the ocean during a severe winter blizzard. She "is comfortable and warm and apparently unconcerned with possible consequences of the storm as she drifts off to sleep. Before dawn she is wrenched into the conscious world, as cruelly as if she had been grabbed by the long hairs of her head." Her heart is pounding against her throat. Her body is hot, but her hands feel cold and clammy. She is in a state of pure panic. It has nothing to do, she reasons, with physical fear. "She was not afraid of being alone, or of being on the dunes in the storm. She was not afraid of bodily attack, rape, all that...She was simply in panic." Mrs. Thayer fights an overwhelming urge to flee by telling herself "It is here [in the house] that I shall survive it or else run out howling across the dunes and die soon in the waves and wind."

It is obvious that Mrs. Thayer's panic has an internal source. To paraphrase Dostoevski in *Notes from the Underground;* no one can live without being able to explain to themselves what is happening to them, and if one day they should no longer be able to explain anything to themselves, they would say they had gone mad, and this would be for them the last explanation left. Dostoevski's sentiment has been echoed by modern-day psychologist Paul Zimbardo, who writes "Most mental illness represents, not a cognitive impairment, but an [attempted] interpretation of discontinuous or inexplicable internal states." Most people regard inexplicable experiences as something which must be explained.

Mrs. Thayer's need to find the source of her panic is a normal biological response to an intense internal arousal. Indeed, the purpose of the orienting response is to identify the unknown in our experience. This is especially important when the unknown may be a threat. When we are unable to correctly identify what is threatening us, all trauma sufferers unwittingly set our own traps.

As Dostoevski and Zimbardo point out, humans have great difficulty in accepting that some aspect of our experience simply cannot be explained. Once the primitive orienting response is invoked, we feel compelled to seek an explanation. When an explanation cannot be found, we usually don't use our powerful cognitive abilities to recognize what is happening. Even if we are able to think clearly, our cognitive powers cannot completely override the primitive need to identify the source of our distress. If, in contrast, the body/mind succeeds in locating the source of its distress (as in the example of Nancy in Chapter Two), the primitive need to identify some source of danger is satisfied. A natural, successful defensive response will then arise to complete the experience. For many of us, this is a giant step toward healing trauma.

Typically, however, we use our cognitive abilities to push the matter further–to figure it out and give it a name (or remember it). In so doing we separate ourselves even further from the experience. In that separateness, the seeds of trauma have fertile ground in which to root and grow. The animal that is unable to locate a source of arousal will freeze rather than flee. When the freezing response begins to override Mrs. Thayer's extreme impulse to flee, she rationalizes (using her neo-cortex) that she will die if she tries to escape the house. She is not only without explanation for her extreme physiological arousal, but she also sets up her own dilemma by convincing herself that if she escapes she will die. Mrs. Thayer then enters into a tight, self-made web of fear-induced immobility.

Like the Chowchilla children (Chapter Two), Mrs. Thayer is more afraid to escape than to remain trapped. Her neo-cortex tries in vain to *explain,* while her reptilian brain compels her to *act.* In the clutch of her terror and self-defeating confusion, Mrs. Thayer will finally focus on her frantic breathing to the exclusion of all else. When she finally suspends her need to understand, she allows her reptilian brain to complete its course of action—that of discharging the extraordinary level of energy that has built up inside of her. We are not told why the energy is there. Perhaps even Mrs Thayer does not consciously know. Fortunately for her (and for us), it does not matter. By focusing on the felt sense of her own breath, Mrs Thayer discharges the energy that was the source of her panic attack.

Can't Synthesize New Information/Can't Learn

An inherent quality of hypervigilance is the absence of the normal orienting responses (Chapter Seven). This has serious ramifications for traumatized people. Primarily, it will impair our overall ability to function effectively in any situation, not just those that require active defense. Part of the function of the orienting response is to identify new information as we become aware of it. If this function is impaired, any amount of new information leads to confusion and overload. Instead of being assimilated and available for future use, new information tends to stack up. It becomes disorganized and unusable. Important pieces of data are misplaced or forgotten. The mind then becomes unable to organize details in a way that makes sense. Rather than retain information that does not make sense, the mind "forgets" it. In the midst of this confusion, any other problem compounds the situation and ordinary circumstances can mushroom into a not-so-comic nightmare of frustration, anger, and anxiety.

For instance, if the lights go off while I am anxiously trying to make sense of the papers on my desk, I am not able to take this unexpected event in stride. I jump, as an irrational thought that someone may be trying to break into my house flashes through my mind. I realize this is probably not true, but my startled movements have knocked a pile of once neatly stacked and vital papers to the floor. Flooded by a sudden surge of irrational anger, I waste energy by pounding the desk in frustrated rage. Unhelpful thoughts barrage me: Is the back door locked? Who was supposed to pay the electric bill? Is Pouncer (my dog) in or out? I find matches and light one, dimly illuminating the messy desk. Where is the electric bill? My attention lapses; I forget that the match is lit and drop it just as it burns my fingers. My papers catch on fire. I feel a sense of terror move through me and I feel paralyzed, unable do anything about the fire. Seconds later, I regain some ability to move but immobility has impaired my motor coordination. I am awkward and ineffective as I flail at the flames. Sensing the danger in my lack of coordination, I become more frantic and realize too late that in my desperation to handle the situation, I have been using the only finished draft of my book to put out the flames. The flames die out on their own. My attempt to make sense of the messy desk begins again. What are all these papers? Did I put this here? Where is the electric bill? I am unable to take in the implications of what I find, and although I have often been offered advice and suggestions by friends and others on how I might get better organized, I continue doing what I have always done. What else can I do? In this state, I am not able to learn, not able to acquire new behaviors, not able to break out of the debilitating patterns which will eventually dominate my life. Without the ability to learn new behaviors, make plans, or synthesize new information, I am deprived of the options available to help me reduce the disarray that threatens to take over my life.

Chronic Helplessness

Chronic helplessness occurs as the freezing, orienting, and defending responses become so fixated and weakened that they move primarily along predetermined and dysfunctional pathways. Chronic helplessness joins hypervigilance and the inability to learn new behaviors as yet another common feature of the traumatized person's reality.

As helplessness becomes an inextricable part of their lives, they will have a difficult time behaving in any way that is not helpless.

All trauma sufferers experience the phenomenon of chronic helplessness to some extent. As a result, we have difficulty participating fully, especially in new situations. For those of us who experience and identify with helplessness, any escape or forward movement is virtually impossible. We become the victims of our own thoughts and self-images. When our physiology responds to an event or stimuli with arousal, we do not move into an orienting and defending response like a healthy human. Instead, we move directly from the arousal into immobility and helplessness, bypassing our other emotions as well as the normal sequence of responses. We become victims, waiting to be victimized again and again.

Without access to normal orienting responses, when threatened we are unable to successfully escape even when the situation offers that possibility. We may not even see it. Arousal is so strongly linked with immobility that the two can't be separated. Arousal leads to immobility. Period. Any time we are aroused, we automatically feel immobilized and helpless. And we are. We may be fortified by adrenaline and physically able to run, but the sense of helplessness is so strong that we are unable to find the exit and leave. This scenario commonly occurs in obsessive relationships; we may know we want out, but fear and immobility override our most primitive connections to the environment, and we stay in spite of ourselves. Instead of normal orienting and defending responses (and the enjoyment and aliveness that are derived from them), we experience anxiety, profound helplessness, shame, numbness, depression, and depersonalization.

Traumatic Coupling

In traumatic coupling, one stimulus is strongly linked to a particular response and together they override normal orienting behaviors. The stimulus engages a specific response. Without exception, we are virtually unable to experience any other outcome. For example, when untraumatized people are given the drug yohimbine, they experience a simple increase in heart rate and blood pressure. In veterans suffering from post-traumatic stress, however, the drug induces a different reaction. Veterans begin re-experiencing the terror and horrors of the battlefield instead of merely experiencing them as physical sensations. This is indicative of traumatic coupling. For veterans, arousal and the emotions that accompany the immobility response—terror, horror, rage and helplessness—are inseparably linked.

A common example of traumatic coupling occurs when traumatized individuals panic when sexually aroused. Sexual arousal leads to panic, immobility and helplessness, rather than intense enjoyment. This may lead people to believe that they have been sexually abused when in fact their reaction is due to traumatic coupling.

Traumatic Anxiety

And no Grand Inquisitor has in readiness such terrible tortures as has anxiety...which never lets him escape, neither by diversion, not by noise, neither at work or at play, neither by day or by night.
—Soren Kierkegaard, Danish philosopher

The aroused state that will not go away, the ongoing

sense of danger, the ceaseless search for that danger, the inability to find it, dissociation, a feeling of helplessness—together, these elements form traumatic anxiety. When we fail to move through the immobility response, the resulting biological message is: "Your life is hanging in the balance." This sense of impending death is intensified by the feelings of rage, terror, panic, and helplessness. All of these factors combine to produce a phenomenon known as traumatic anxiety.

The word "fear" comes from the Old English term for danger, while "anxious" is derived rom the Greek root word meaning to "press tight" or strangle.

The experience of traumatic anxiety is profound. It goes far beyond the experience we usually equate with anxiety. The elevated state of arousal, the symptoms, the fear of exiting or fully entering the immobility state, as well as a nagging awareness that something is very wrong, produce an almost-constant state of extreme anxiety. This anxiousness serves as the backdrop for all experience in the severely traumatized person's life. Just as we are more aware of the water than the fish that swims in it, so may anxiety be more apparent to those around traumatized people than it is to them. Traumatic anxiety displays itself as nervousness, fretting and worrying, and in appearing to be "high-strung." The sufferer frequently experiences panic, dread, and highly overdramatized reactions to trivial events. These maladies are not permanent fixtures of the personality, but are indicative of a nervous system temporarily, though perpetually, overwhelmed.

Psychosomatic Symptoms

Traumatic symptoms not only affect our emotional and mental states, but our physical health as well. When no other cause for a physical malady can be found, stress and trauma are likely candidates. Trauma can make a person blind, mute, or deaf; it can cause paralysis in legs, arms, or both; it can bring about chronic neck and back pain, chronic fatigue syndrome, bronchitis, asthma, gastrointestinal problems, severe PMS, migraines, and a whole host of so-called psychosomatic conditions. Any physical system capable of binding the undischarged arousal caused by trauma is fair game. The trapped energy will use any aspect of our physiology available to it.

Denial

Many trauma sufferers live in a state of resignation regarding their symptoms, without ever attempting to find a way back to a more normal, healthy life. Denial and amnesia play an important role in reinforcing this resigned state. Though we may be tempted to judge or criticize people who deny that they have been traumatized (claiming that nothing really happened), it is important to remember that this (in itself) is a symptom. Denial and amnesia are not volitional choices that the person makes; they do not indicate weakness of character, personality dysfunction, or deliberate dishonesty. This dysfunctional pathway becomes patterned in our physiology. At the time of a traumatic event, denial helps preserve the ability to function and survive. However, when chronic, denial becomes a maladaptive symptom of trauma.

Reversing the effects of either denial or amnesia takes a great deal of courage. The amount of energy that is released when this happens can be tremendous and should not be minimized or underestimated. It is a time of great significance for the traumatized person.

Gladys

Gladys' story may seem ludicrous, but it is true and well within the range of experience that one might expect with typical denial. The process of coming out of denial or amnesia can be facilitated by the support of family, friends, and therapists, but the proper time for this awakening is purely a biological and physiological matter.

Gladys was referred to me by her doctor, who was treating her for thyroid problems. The internist had been unable to ascertain a physical reason for her recurring attacks of acute abdominal pain. Upon meeting her for the first time, I was struck by her intense, fearful, open-eyed appearance. Her eyes seemed to pop out of her head, a classic indicator not only of hyperthyroidism, but also of fear and chronic hypervigilance. I asked her whether she felt fearful or had ever experienced trauma. She told me that she had not.

Knowing that people sometimes deny trauma, I rephrased my question and asked her whether she had experienced anything that was especially frightening or upsetting in the last five years. Again, she answered no. In an attempt to increase her comfort, I commented that a recent study had found that a large percentage of the population had experienced something frightening within the last five years.

"Oh, really," she responded. "Well, I was kidnapped a few years ago. But it wasn't that frightening."

"Not even a little?"

"No, not really."

"What happened?"

"Well, I was skiing in Colorado with some friends and we were supposed to go out to dinner. A man drove up, opened his door, and I got in. But he didn't go to the restaurant."

"Were you scared then?"

"No, it was a ski weekend."

"Where did he go?"

"He took me to his house."

"Weren't you scared when he didn't go to the restaurant and took you to his house instead?"

"No, I didn't know why he was taking me there."

"Oh. Well, what happened then?"

"He tied me up to his bed."

"Was that scary?"

"No, nothing really happened. He just threatened me. Well, maybe I was scared a little bit. He had all kinds of knives and guns hanging on his walls."

"But you weren't really scared?"

"No, nothing happened."

Gladys left that day with an outwardly calm demeanor. Her claim that she had not been frightened during the kidnapping or at any other time still dominated her experience. She did not return.

Gladys' story, while extreme, is typical of denial. Denial keeps the traumatized person in its grip until the primitive processes that guard the system decide to let go. We may come out of denial because we feel safe, because another event triggers a "memory," or because our biologys say, "Enough." While there are things that friends, loved ones, and therapists can do to help (i.e., intervention), a sensitivity to timing is critical to the success of these approaches.

What Trauma Survivors Expect

The young girl whose father molests her will freeze in her bed because she cannot escape the terror and shame of the experience by running away. In having her active defensive escape response thwarted, the child's ability to orient to normal stimuli will change. She will no longer respond with curiosity and expectancy. Her actions will be constricted and frozen in fear. The sound of footsteps, which the "normal" child orients to with alert expectancy, evokes frozen terror in the incest child.

When the incest is ongoing, the child responds by becoming habitually frozen in the immobility state. For children who are threatened, however, immobility becomes a dysfunctional symptom of their trauma. Children become both psychological and physiological victims, and will carry that posture throughout their lives. They will be unable to make a full switch from immobility back to the possibility of active escape, regardless of the situation they find themselves in. They become so identified with helplessness and shame that they literally no longer have the resources to defend themselves when attacked or put under pressure.

All humans who are repeatedly overwhelmed become identified with states of anxiety and helplessness. In addition, they bring this helplessness to many other situations that are perceived as threats. They make the "decision" that they are helpless, and continue in many varied ways to prove this victimization to themselves and to others. They give in to the helpless feelings even in situations that they have the resources to master. Sometimes (in what is known as a counter-phobic reaction), they may attempt to disprove what they don't like about themselves by deliberately provoking danger. Either way, they are behaving as victims and their behaviors propagate further victimization.

Career criminals speak of using body language to choose their victims. They have learned through experience that certain people do not defend themselves as well as others. What they look for are the telltale signs revealed in the stiff, uncoordinated movements and the disoriented behavior of their potential prey.

The Last Turn

As trauma symptoms grow more complex, they begin incorporating all the aspects of the trauma sufferer's experience into their web. These symptoms have a physiological basis, but by the time their development has reached the last turn in its downward spiral, they will be not only affecting, but actually driving the mental aspects of our experience as well. What is most frightening is that a large portion of this impact will remain unconscious.

The impact of trauma may not be fully conscious but it certainly is fully active. In an insidious way, trauma contributes to the motives and drives of our behavior. What this means is that the man who was hit as a child will feel compelled to hit as an adult. The energy behind his need to strike out is none other than the energy contained in his traumatic symptoms. This unconscious compulsion can only be conquered by great acts of will until the energy is discharged.

The phenomenon that drives the repetition of past traumatic events is called re-enactment. It is the symptom that dominates the last turn of the downward spiral in the development of trauma symptoms. Re-enactment is more compelling, mysterious, and destructive to us as individuals, as a society, and as a world community.

III
Transformation

13
Blueprint for Repetition

Re-Enactment

It astonishes us far too little.
—Sigmund Freud

The drive to complete and heal trauma is as powerful and tenacious as the symptoms it creates. The urge to resolve trauma through re-enactment can be severe and compulsive. We are inextricably drawn into situations that replicate the original trauma in both obvious and unobvious ways. The prostitute or "stripper" with a history of childhood sexual abuse is a common example. We may find ourselves experiencing the effects of trauma either through physical symptoms or through a full-blown interaction with the external environment. Re-enactments may be acted out in intimate relationships, work situations, repetitive accidents or mishaps, and in other seemingly random events. They may also appear in the form of bodily symptoms or psychosomatic diseases. Children who have had a traumatic experience will often repeatedly recreate it in their play. Adults, on a larger developmental scale, will re-enact traumas in our daily lives. The mechanism is similar regardless of the individual's age.

From a biological perspective, behavior that is as powerful and compelling as re-enactment falls into the category of "survival strategies." This means that the behaviors have been selected because, historically, they are advantageous to the perpetuation of a species. What, then, is the survival value of the often dangerous re-enactments that plague many traumatized individuals and societies?

When it comes to survival knowledge, we must learn about and from our environment quickly and effectively. It is essential that the desire to learn and relearn be compelling. In the wild, a young animal's initial escapes are often "beginner's luck." It must develop behaviors that increase the likelihood of escape, therefore the education period is quick and intense.

In order to enhance this learning process, I believe that animals "review" each close encounter and practice possible escape options *after* the aroused survival energy is discharged. I saw an example of this behavior on the Discovery Channel. Three cheetah cubs had narrowly escaped a pursuing lion by quickly changing their course and climbing high into a tree. After the lion departed, the cubs shinnied down and began to play. Each cub took a turn playing the lion while the other two practiced different escape maneuvers. They practiced zigging and zagging, then scurrying up the tree until their mother returned from a hunting excursion. Then, they proudly pranced around mom, informing her of their empowering escape from death's mighty jaws.

I believe that the biological taproot of re-enactment occurs in this "second phase" of normalization—the "playful" practice of defensive strategies. How can this innately playful survival mechanism degenerate into an often tragic, pathological, and violent traumatic re-enactment? This is an important question for us to answer, not only for individual trauma sufferers, but for society as a whole. Much of the violence that plagues humanity is a direct or indirect result of unresolved trauma that is acted out in repeated unsuccessful attempts to re-establish a sense of empowerment..

The cheetah cubs discharged most of the intense survival energy they had mobilized during their successful escape from the lion (phase one). After the escape, they appeared exhilarated. Then, they entered phase two—they began to "playfully" review the experience which led them towards mastery, and perhaps to feelings of pride and empowerment.

Let's look at a more human scenario: while driving, you see a car coming directly toward you. *Your body instinctively mobilizes to defend itself. As you zig-zag out of harm's way, you feel an intense energy discharge. You notice that the car is a Mercury Cougar. You feel exhilarated by your successful escape. You pull over to the curb and notice that although you have discharged much energy, you still feel somewhat activated. You focus your awareness on the felt sense, and notice minute trembling in your jaws and pelvis which spreads throughout your body. You feel warmth and tingling in your arms and hands as the energy discharges. Feeling calmer now, you begin to review the event. You "play out" different scenarios of the situation and decide that your defensive strategy, although successful, could have been done in other ways. You make a note of these alternatives, and begin to relax. You drive home and tell your family what happened. There is pride in your demeanor, and you feel empowered by the re-telling of the event. Your family is supportive and glad you are safe. You are deeply touched by their concern, and feel their welcoming arms around you. You suddenly feel tired and decide to take a nap before dinner. You are calm and relaxed, and drift off immediately. When you awaken, you feel revitalized. The event is history, and you are ready to engage life with your usual sense of self.*

Unfortunately, humans often do not completely discharge the vast energies mobilized to protect themselves. Thus, when they enter the second phase, they are reviewing the event, but remain in a highly aroused state. This heightened energy level will not allow the "playful" reviewing to occur. Instead, they may experience often terrifying and compulsive flashbacks that are akin to reliving the event. In Chapter Sixteen, *Scenario of Healing from an Accident,* the most common response to incomplete discharge is addressed. A majority of people attempt to control their undischarged survival energy by internalizing it. Although this approach is more socially acceptable, it is no less violent than "acting out." It is also no more effective in dealing with the highly charged activation. It is important for us to understand that the strategy of internalizing instinctive defensive procedures is a form of re-enactment—perhaps it could be called "acting in." To commit violence on oneself is the method preferred by our culture for several reasons. Obviously, it is easier to maintain a social structure that appears to be in control of itself. However, I think there is another, more compelling reason—by internalizing our natural propensity to resolve life-threatening events, we are denying that the need even exists—it remains hidden. One of the positive aspects in the recent escalation of violent "acting out" is that it is forcing us to face the fact that post traumatic stress, whether it manifests as "acting in" or "acting out," is a major health issue. Let's look at an "acted out" scenario:

While driving, you see a car coming directly toward you. Your body tenses instantly, then freezes as you feel panic. You brace yourself, feeling resigned to the unavoidable impact.

You feel that you have lost control...then, at the last micro-second, you fight off the panic, and swerve out of the path of the oncoming car. As you pass by, you notice that the car is a Mercury Cougar. You pull over to the curb, and stop the car. Your heart is pounding wildly, and you are gasping for breath. As you try to regain control, you have a fleeting moment of "adrenaline rush," followed by the intense sensation of high arousal. You are frightened by this energy, and feel yourself becoming angry. The anger helps. You focus your rage on the idiot that almost got you killed. Heart and mind still racing, you notice your ice-cold hands are still glued to the steering wheel. You imagine strangling the idiot with all your might. Still wound up, images of the event begin to flash before your eyes. (the second phase begins, but you are still highly charged). The panicky feeling returns, and your heart beats rapidly. You are losing control, and you feel the anger return. Anger has become your friend—it helps you maintain some semblance of control.

Your thoughts return to the idiot. He has ruined your day. You wonder if he is going through the same thing you are. You doubt that he is, because he's such an idiot. He probably just went on his merry way, oblivious to the whole incident. You hate that possibility, but begin to think that it's true. Then you get a flash—you remember the car—it was a yellow Cougar. Your anger swells at the vision of it. You hate the car and its driver. You are going to teach them both a lesson.

You drive down the street in search of the yellow cougar. You spot it in a parking lot. Your heart races and your excite-ment mounts as you turn into the lot. Revenge will be yours—justice will be served. You park a few cars away, open your trunk, and grab the tire iron. In a rush of energy, you head directly for the Cougar and begin smashing the wind-shield with the tire iron. You smash and smash, again and again, trying to discharge the intense energy. Suddenly, you stop and look around. People are staring at you in disbelief.

Some of them are afraid of you, others think you are nuts, others are giving you hostile glares. For a split second, you consider attacking the hostile ones. They are probably friends of the Cougar owner. Then, reality sinks in. You realize what you have done, and are overcome with shame. The shame is immediately replaced by panic. You have broken the law, and the police are probably on their way. It is time to escape. You run to your car, get in, and drive off, leaving a cloud of burnt rubber.

By the time you arrive home, the shame has overtaken you. Your family is glad to see you, but you cannot tell them what happened. They ask you what is wrong, but you dismiss them. The temporary relief at smashing the windshield is long gone. It has been replaced, once again, by the panic. You can't stay at home. You get into the car and drive, trying to calm yourself. Nothing seems to work. You tell yourself that the idiot deserved what he got, but you enjoy little relief from the thought. You decide you need help to relax, and head for the nearest bar.

Obviously, this response has very little survival value. The person in the above scenario could not review the event intelligently in a highly aroused state. Instead of becoming empowered, this condition led him to re-enact or "act out" his biological confusion rather than discharge the survival energy and return to normal functioning. It is important to refrain from judgment of this particular type of response. We must see it for what it truly is—*an unsuccessful attempt to discharge the intense energy mobilized to defend against a perceived life-threatening experience.* Psychiatrist James Gilligan, in his book *Violence*[8], makes this eloquent statement: ..."*the attempt to achieve and maintain justice, or to undo or prevent injustice, is the one and only universal cause of violence.*" (italics his) On an emotional and intellectual level, Dr. Gilligan's insight is profound and accurate, but how does

---

[8]Grosset–Putnam. 1996, p. 11

it translate into the biological level of instinctive functioning? To the non-thinking world of the felt sense, I believe that justice is experienced as completion. Without discharge and completion, we are doomed to repeat the tragic cycle of violent re-enactment, whether it be through "acting out" or "acting in."

It is humbling to own up to the fact that a significant portion of human behavior is performed from hyper-aroused states due to incomplete responses to threat. Most of humanity appears to be fascinated, perhaps even mesmerized by those of us who "act out" our search for justice. There are countless books detailing the lives of "serial-killers," many of them best-sellers. The theme of justice and revenge is probably the subject of more movies than any other single topic.

Underlying our powerful attraction to those who "act out" is the urge for completion and resolution—or, what I call "renegotiation" of trauma. In a renegotiation, the repetitive cycle of violent re-enactment is transformed into a healing event. A transformed person feels no need for revenge or violence—shame and blame dissolve in the powerful wake of renewal and self-acceptance (see Chapter Fourteen – *Transformation*). Unfortunately, there are very few examples of this phenomenon in literature and films. The movie *Sling Blade* has many of the transformative qualities inherent in a traumatic renegotiation.

Our mundane "collision scenario" is much more a part of everyday life than the stuff movies are made of, and therefore, more telling. On page 133 of *Violence,* Gilligan writes: "If we want to understand the nature of the incident that typically provokes the most intense shame, and hence the most extreme violence, we need to recognize that it is precisely the triviality of the incident that makes the incident so shameful. And it is the intensity of the shame, as I said, that makes the incident so powerfully productive of violence." When people are overwhelmed and cannot successfully defend themselves, they often feel ashamed. When they act violently, they are seeking justice and vengeance for having been shamed.

In Chapter Seven, we discussed the fact that the human brain has three integral systems: reptilian (instincts), mammalian (emotions), and neo-cortex (rational). Shame is an emotion formulated by the (mammalian) brain system. Justice is an idea formulated by the neo-cortex, but what of the instincts? It is my contention that if the instinctive urge to discharge intense survival energy is thwarted, then the function of the other two brain systems is profoundly altered. For example, let's look at the previously mentioned "re-enactment" scenario. What effect did the undischarged energy have on the emotional and rational responses of the individual? Quite simply, the emotional brain translated this energy into anger. Then, the "rational" brain created the idea of revenge. These two inter-related systems were doing what they could, given the circumstances. However, the failure to instinctively discharge a very powerful biological energy put them in a position they are not adapted to handle. The result of this attempt—re-enactment rather than renegotiation.

Although violent behavior may provide temporary relief and an increased feeling of "pride", without biological discharge, there is no completion. As a result, the cycle of shame and violence returns. The nervous system remains highly activated, which compels people to seek the only relief they know—more violence. The traumatic event is not resolved, and people continue to behave as if it is still happening—because, biologically speaking, it is—their nervous systems are still highly activated. The three little cheetah cubs mentioned earlier knew when the real event was over. The human being, with its vastly "superior" intelligence, often does not.

Struck by the way in which people's entire lives seem to play out themes from their childhood, Freud coined the term "repetition compulsion" to describe the behaviors, relationships, emotions, and dreams that seemed to be replays of early trauma. Central to Freud's concept of repetition compulsion was his observation that people continue to put themselves in situations strangely reminiscent of an original trauma in order to learn new solutions.

July 5th, 6:30 in the Morning

Bessel van der Kolk, a psychiatric researcher who has made great contributions to the field of post-traumatic stress, relates a story about a veteran that illustrates vividly both the dangerous and repetitive aspects of re-encactment in its drive toward resolution.

On July 5 in the late 1980's a man walked into a convenience store at 6:30 in the morning. Holding his finger in his pocket to simulate a gun, he demanded that the cashier give him the contents of the cash register. Having collected about five dollars in change, the man returned to his car, where he remained until the police arrived. When the police arrived, the young man got out of his car and, with his finger again in his pocket, announced that he had a gun and that everyone should stay away from him. Luckily, he was taken into custody without being shot.

At the police station, the officer who looked up the man's record discovered that he had committed six other so-called "armed robberies" over the past fifteen years—all of them at 6:30 in the morning on July 5!

Upon learning that the man was a Vietnam veteran, the police surmised that this event was more than mere coincidence. They took him to a nearby VA hospital, where Dr. van der Kolk had the opportunity to speak with him.

Van der Kolk asked the man directly: "What happened to you on July 5th at 6:30 in the morning?" He responded directly. While he was in Vietnam, the man's platoon had been ambushed by the Viet Cong. Everyone had been killed except for himself and his friend, Jim. The date was July fourth. Darkness fell and the helicopters were unable to evacuate them. They spent a terrifying night together huddled in a rice paddy surrounded by the Viet Cong. At about 3:30 in the morning, Jim was hit in the chest by a Viet Cong bullet; he died in his friend's arms at 6:30 on the morning of July 5.

After returning to the States, every July 5 (that he did not spend in jail), the man had re-enacted the anniversary of his friend's death. In the therapy session with van der Kolk, the vet experienced grief over the loss of his friend. He then made the connection between Jim's death and the compulsion he felt to commit the robberies. Once he became aware of his feelings and the role the original event had played in driving his compulsion, the man was able to stop re-enacting this tragic incident.

What was the connection between the robberies and the Vietnam experience? By staging the "robberies," the man was recreating the firefight that had resulted in the death of his friend (as well as the rest of his platoon). By provoking the police to join in the re-enactment, the vet had orchestrated the cast of characters needed to play the role of the Viet Cong. He did not want to hurt anyone, so he used his fingers instead of a gun. He then brought the situation to a climax and was able to elicit the help he needed to heal his psychic wounds. He was then able to resolve his anguish, grief, and guilt about his buddy's violent death and the horrors of war.

If we look at this man's behaviors without knowing anything about his past, we might think he was mad. However, with a little history, we can see that his actions were a brilliant attempt to resolve a deep emotional scar. His re-enactment took him to the very edge, again and again, until he was finally able to free himself from the overwhelming nightmare of war.

In many so-called primitive cultures, the nature of this man's emotional and spiritual injuries would be openly acknowledged by the tribe. He would be encouraged to share his pain. A healing ceremony would be performed in the presence of the whole village. With the help of his people, the man would re-unite with his lost spirit. After this cleansing, in a joyous celebration, the man would be welcomed back as a hero.

The Vital Role of Awareness

The link between a re-enactment and the original situation may not be readily obvious. A traumatized person may associate the traumatic event with another situation and repeat that situation instead of the original one. Recurring accidents are one common way this type of re-enactment occurs, especially when the accidents are similar in some way. In other cases, the person may continue to incur a particular type of injury. Sprained ankles, wrenched knees, whiplash, and even many so-called psychosomatic diseases are common examples of physical re-enactments.

Commonly, none of these so-called "accidents" appear to be anything but accidents. The clue to identifying them as symptoms of trauma lies in how often they are repeated and the frequency with which they occur. One young man, sexually abused as a child, had over a dozen serious rear-end collisions within a period of three years. (In none of these "accidents" was he obviously at fault.) Frequent re-enactment is the most intriguing and complex symptom of trauma. This phenomenon can be custom-fit to the individual, with a startling level of "coincidence" between the re-enactment and the original situation. While some of the elements of re-enactment are understandable, others seem to defy rational explanation.

Jack

Jack is a very shy and serious man in his mid-fifties who lives in the Northwest. He is quite embarrassed about his reason for seeing me. However, underneath this embarrassment is a pervasive sense of humiliation and defeat. Last summer while docking his boat, he proudly and playfully announced to his wife, "Is this a beautiful job or what?" The next moment he, his wife, and their child found themselves on their backs. What happened was, that as he was mooring the boat, one of the lines got caught in the throttle-clutch. Suddenly, the boat lurched forward. (He had left the motor idling in neutral while mooring it.) Jack and his family were jerked off their feet. Fortunately, no one was seriously hurt, but he smashed into another boat causing $5,000 worth of damage. Adding insult to injury, the completely humiliated Jack got into a shouting match with the marina owner when the man (probably thinking that Jack was drunk) insisted on docking the boat for him. Being an experienced boatman from a nautical family, this episode had more than knocked the wind out of him. Jack had known better than to let the engine idle while docking.

Through the felt sense, he is able to experience holding the rope and feeling it wrench across his burning arms before he falls on his back. This stimulates an image of himself at age five. While boating with his parents, he fell off a ladder onto his back. The wind was knocked out of him, and he was terrified because he could not breathe.

In exploring this experience, he vividly senses his powerful five-year-old muscles gripping onto the ladder as he proudly climbs it. His parents, being otherwise occupied, don't see him playing on the ladder. When a large wave tips the boat, Jack is thrown on his back. In a humiliating sequel, he is taken from doctor to doctor, repeating the story to each.

There is an important relationship between these two events—the fall at age five and his recent fiasco. In both instances he is proudly displaying his prowess in play. In both events he is thrown on his back, having the wind literally and emotionally knocked out of him. His father's boat was called *The High Seas*. A week prior to the mishap Jack had christened his boat *The High Seas*.

Patterns of Shock

When Jack renamed his boat *The High Seas* he, like the Vietnam vet, was setting the stage for the re-enactment that subsequently occurred. Coincidental reminders of incidents frequently occur just prior to a re-enactment. What is even more remarkable is that to an uninvolved observer, these incidents and the subsequent re-enactments may clearly be seen as relating to the original trauma. However, the traumatized person usually has no inkling of it.

Often, a reenactment will coincide not with unconscious incidental reminders, but with the anniversary of a traumatic event. This may be true even though the individual has no conscious memory that the event ever occurred! Even for those who remember the event, the link between the original experience and the re-enactment is typically unconscious. Indeed, as we will see, lack of conscious awareness plays a key role in perpetuating these often-bizarre reruns.

Without Awareness We Have No Choice

Try ridding your yard of ivy, blackberry bushes, or bamboo by cutting them off at the ground. Anyone who has attempted this knows it can't be done. Some things must be dealt with at the roots. Trauma is one of these things. When re-enactments occur, we often refer to the resulting behavior as "acting out." These words are well chosen. It is called acting out because it isn't real. Something else is really at the root of it—something that the person isn't aware of.

As we discussed earlier, acting out does offer the organism some temporary relief. The actions themselves provide an outlet for excess energy generated by the ongoing arousal cycle. Adrenaline-forming chemicals and narcotic endorphins are released into the body. At the same time the organism is able to avoid feeling the overwhelming emotion and sensation that would accompany the real thing. The drawback is that by going with the programmed act, the person rarely has a chance to try anything new or original. Few rational people would choose to live their lives in the grips of trauma by constantly acting out and reliving overwhelming experiences.

Re-enactment Versus Renegotiation

In any re-enactment there will always be underlying and unconscious patterns of events and beliefs that seemingly have their own power to create our experiences according to their dictates. This compulsive repetition is not "deliberate" in the usual sense. Deliberate actions usually require some consciousness, an ingredient that plays little role in re-enactment. In re-enactments, the human organism is not fully aware of the drives and motivations of its behavior, and consequently, it operates in a mode that is like that of the reptilian brain. It simply does what it does.

Re-enactment represents the organism's attempt to complete the natural cycle of activation and deactivation that accompanies the response to threat in the wild. In the wild, activation is often discharged by running or fighting—or by other active behaviors that bring about a successful conclusion to the potentially life-threatening confrontation. If the original event required an active escape strategy, then reenactments that attempt the same thing should come as no surprise to us.

Because we are human, we are vulnerable to traumatization in a way that animals are not. The key to the exit from this seemingly unsolvable predicament lies in the characteristic that most clearly distinguishes us from animals—our ability to be *consciously* aware of our inner experience. When we are able, as Jack was, to *slow down* and experience all the elements of sensation and feeling that accompany our traumatic patterns, allowing them to complete themselves before we move on, we begin to access and transform the drives and motivations that otherwise compel us to re-enact traumatic events. Conscious awareness accessed through the felt sense provides us with a gentle energetic discharge just as effective as that which the animal accesses through action. This is *renegotiation.*

In the Theater of the Body

Arousal becomes chronic as a result of overwhelming sensations and emotions that have an internal source. This is the reason that trauma can and must be transformed by working with it internally. In re-enactment the world may be our stage. In remaining external, it also remains unchanged. Hence, re-enactment rarely accomplishes its intended task.

It is to our detriment that we live in a culture that does not honor the internal world. In many cultures, the internal world of dreams, feelings, images, and sensations is sacred. Yet, most of us are only peripherally aware of its existence. We have little or no experience of finding our way around in this internal landscape. Consequently, when our experience demands it, we are unprepared. Rather than negotiating it skillfully, if we attempt it at all, we are more likely to re-enact it.

With patience and attention, however, the patterns that drive traumatic re-enactment can be dismantled so that we again access the infinite, feeling tones and behavioral responses that we are capable of executing. Once we understand how trauma begins and develops, we must then learn to know ourselves through the felt sense. All the information that we need to begin renegotiating trauma is available to us. Our bodies (instincts) will tell us where the blockages are and when we are moving too fast. Our intellects can tell us how to regulate the experience so that we are not overwhelmed. When these brain functions work as one, we can establish a special relationship between the mainstream for our internal experience and the turmoil of trauma. Moving slowly and allowing the experience to unfold at each step allows us to digest the unassimilated aspects of the traumatic experience at a rate that we are able to tolerate.

In the theater of the body, trauma can be transformed. The fragmented elements that perpetuate traumatic emotion and behavior can be completed, integrated, and made whole again. Along with this wholeness comes a sense of mastery and resolution.

Postscript: How Far in Time and Space?

No discussion of re-enactment would be complete without at least an acknowledgment of one intriguing aspect of traumatic repetition that defies explanation. Specifically, I am referring to re-enactments of traumatic events that can be tracked back through several generations of a family's history.

In a training class, I was recently asked to see a young woman, "Kelly," who had been in the Sioux City airplane disaster (upon which the movie *Fearless* was based). The flight, en route from Denver to Chicago, lost an engine in an explosive blast. The plane tilted and plummeted downward at an angle so steep that a tailspin seemed unavoidable. Remarkably, the pilot, Al Haynes, kept the plane from going into a tailspin and was able to make an emergency landing. Upon impact, the plane split apart. Pieces of the burning fuselage were strewn into the surrounding cornfields. This dramatic event was recorded by one of the decade's most famous amateur videographers. Kelly had escaped being trapped in a crushed section of the aircraft by crawling through a twisted maze of metal and wires toward a spot of light.

As we work together, Kelly slowly and gradually renegotiates the horror of the crash. When we move into the portion of her experience that occurred at the time of the impact, Kelly hears the voice of her father and grandfather shouting: "Don't wait; go now! Go to the light. Get out before the fireball." She obeyed. Both Kelly's father and grandfather had survived separate plane crashes. Both men had narrowly escaped death by leaving the wreckage as soon as the plane hit the ground.

It is likely Kelly had heard stories about the experiences of her father and grandfather, and these stories may well have helped her know what to do when the plane came down. But what about the other elements of the experience? Plane crashes receive a great deal of media coverage. They often affect the lives of hundreds of people at a time, but on the whole, not many of us have even one family member who has been in a plane crash, let alone three. Further, there is the nature of the event to consider. An automobile accident can fairly easily be attributed to a moment of unconsciousness, even one in which the unaware individual seems not to be at fault. It goes far beyond probability to suggest that a plane crash can occur in a similar way.

I have heard several stories of a similar nature from clients and friends. Events occur over generations that have startlingly coincidental elements. In some cases, these coincidences can be at least partially attributed to ways the child was shaped by family myths and patterns. Others (particularly when large groups of people are involved in a disaster of this magnitude) cannot be explained. I leave further comment to Rod Serling, but not without wondering how far the patterns of traumatic shock truly extend.

Another example of the mysterious ways of traumatic re-enactment is found in the story of Jessica. At age two, she survived her first plane crash. The pilot, her father, held her in his arms and carried her down from the tree in which the small craft had landed. Twenty-five years later, flying nine hundred miles from home, Jessica and her boyfriend got lost in a blizzard and crashed into a tree. The tree, it turned out, was just on the other side of the same hill where she had crashed as a two-year-old! In our session together, she resolved many deep feelings and responses from a complex and difficult childhood. Does this mean that she has no need for another accident—or that the second crash into that hill was anything but a coincidence—I just don't know, and hope I never will; chalk it up to the mystery of it all.

The reason we are united in spirit to both Heaven and Hell is to keep us in freedom.
—Emanuel Swedenborg

14

Transformation

For a traumatized person, the journey toward a vital, spontaneous life means more than alleviating symptoms—it means transformation. When we successfully renegotiate trauma, a fundamental shift occurs in our beings. Transformation is the process of changing something in relation to its polar opposite. In the transformation between a traumatic state and a peaceful state, there are fundamental changes in our nervous systems, feelings, and perceptions that are experienced through the felt sense. The nervous system swings between immobility and fluidity, emotions fluctuate between fear and courage, and perceptions shift between narrow-mindedness and receptivity.

Through transformation, the nervous system regains its capacity for self-regulation. Our emotions begin to lift us up rather than bring us down. They propel us into the exhilarating ability to soar and fly, giving us a more complete view of our place in nature. Our perceptions broaden to encompass a receptivity and acceptance of what is, without judgment. We are able to learn from our life experiences. Without trying to forgive, we understand that there is no blame. We often obtain a surer sense of self while becoming more resilient and spontaneous. This new self-assuredness allows us to relax, enjoy, and live life more fully. We become more in tune with the passionate and ecstatic dimensions of life.

This is a profound metamorphosis—a change that affects the most basic levels of our beings. We will no longer view our world through fearful eyes. Though our planet can be a dangerous place, we will no longer suffer from the constant fear that creates hypervigilance—a feeling that danger always lurks and the worst often happens. We begin to face life with a developing sense of courage and trust. The world becomes a place where bad things may happen but they can be overcome. Trust, rather than anxiety, forms the field in which all experience occurs. Transformation ripples out into every corner of our lives, much like the debilitating effects of trauma once did. Tim Cahill, the adventurer and writer, puts it this way, "I put my life on the line to save my soul."[9] In trauma we have already put our lives on the line, but the reward of salvation is yet to be claimed.

Two Faces of Trauma

Pieces of a burning fuselage are strewn over a large cornfield scarred by a blackened path of destruction. In this dramatic opening scene from Peter Weir's extraordinary film, *Fearless*, Max Klein (played by Jeff Bridges) has just survived a commercial airline crash. He staggers through giant stalks of corn, holding an infant limply in one arm and leading a ten-year-old child with the other. As paramedics and firemen rush around, Max hails a taxi and asks to be taken to a motel. Conveying an eerie sense of numbness, he showers. Under the stream of water, he searches with his hands to reassure himself that he still has a body. He is surprised when he discov-

---

[9] Jaguars Ripped My Flesh—Adventure is a Risky Business, Bantam Books, 1987

ers a deep gash in his side. The next morning, Max, who had been phobic about flying before the crash, refuses an offer to ride the train home. Cockily, this (now) ex-neurotic opts for a first-class upgrade on a return flight.

Once home, Max loses interest in the mundane reality of daily living. He drifts away from his family and the material world, and soon plunges into a dizzying romance with a fellow survivor (played by Rosie Perez). Irrevocably changed, he no longer fears death. Worshipped as a hero by those whose lives he has saved, Max—fearless—has apparently been transformed. But has he?

In this truly complex film, two sides of trauma are portrayed. Max's life has been changed profoundly by his heroic actions in the face of death. However, he has changed in two different and contradictory ways. On the one hand, he appears to have "transcended" the ordinary world, and entered an expanded, gloriously passionate existence. At the same time, he has become constricted and is no longer able to tolerate or experience his normal life. He becomes increasingly wound-up in an ever-tightening spiral that literally spins him into life-threatening re-enactments of the trauma. In a wild attempt to heal his new lover, he almost kills them both. Ultimately, it is through her compassionate love that Max snaps out of his "messianic" delusion and confronts his own terror and desperate need to be saved.

Every trauma provides an opportunity for authentic transformation. Trauma amplifies and evokes the expansion and contraction of psyche, body, and soul. It is how we respond to a traumatic event that determines whether trauma will be a cruel and punishing Medusa turning us into stone, or whether it will be a spiritual teacher taking us along vast and uncharted pathways. In the Greek myth, blood from Medusa's slain body was taken in two vials; one vial had the power to kill, while the other had the power to resurrect. If we let it, trauma has the power to rob our lives of vitality and destroy it. However, we can also use it for powerful self-renewal and transformation. Trauma, *resolved,* is a blessing from a greater power.

Heaven, Hell, and Healing: A Middle Ground

The great way is not difficult for he who has no preferences; but make the slightest distinction and Heaven and Hell are set infinitely apart
—Hsin Hsin Ming (the Forrest Gump of the third Century)

In *Fearless,* Max wobbles between heavenly rapture and hellish nightmare in an ever-constricting vortex of energy. This buffeting between the extreme polarities of heaven and hell generates the rhythm essential for the transformation of trauma. Finally, in surrendering to his own need to be saved, Max goes to the threshold of death's door. While he was fortunate enough to transform his trauma without literally getting killed or going crazy, there are less violent, more dependable methods available for transformation.

Somatic Experiencing is one these methods. It allows us to gradually bridge the chasm between "heaven" and "hell," uniting the two polarities. Physiologically speaking, heaven is expansion and hell is contraction. With their gradual unification, trauma is gently healed.

Organisms have evolved exquisite processes to heal the effects of trauma. These processes include the ability to unite, integrate, and transform the polarities of expansion and contraction. If these polarities are integrated in a gradual fashion, then trauma can be safely healed. When dealing with a physical trauma, the physician's job is to support healing (wash the wound, protect it with a bandage or cast, etc.). The cast doesn't heal the broken bone; it provides the physical mechanism of support that allows the bone to initiate and complete its own intelligent healing processes. Similarly, in integrating the psychic polarities of expansion and contraction, the felt sense supports us in orchestrating the marvel of transformation.

Let It Flow—Renegotiation

Everything flows, out and in; everything has its tides;
all things rise and fall; the pendulum-swing manifests
in everything; the measure of the swing to the right is
the measure of the swing to the left; rhythm compensates.
—The Kybalion

Our lives are like streams. The currents of our experiences flow through time with periodic cycles of tranquillity, disturbance, and integration. Our bodies are the banks of the stream, containing our life-energy and holding it in bounds while allowing it to freely flow within the banks. It is the protective barrier of the bank that allows us to safely experience our sense of inner movement and change. Freud, in 1914, defined trauma "...as a breach in the protective barrier against stimuli leading to feelings of overwhelming helplessness."[10] Using the analogy of the stream, shock trauma can be visualized as an external force rupturing the protective container (banks) of our experience. This breach then creates a turbulent vortex. With the rupture, an explosive rushing out of life-energy creates a trauma vortex. This whirlpool exists outside the banks of our life stream of normal experience (Fig. 2). It is common for traumatized individuals either to get sucked into the trauma vortex or to avoid the breach entirely by staying distanced from the region where the breach (trauma) occurred.

---

[10] from Lectures, and Beyond the Pleasure Principle, International Psycho-Analytic Press, 1922

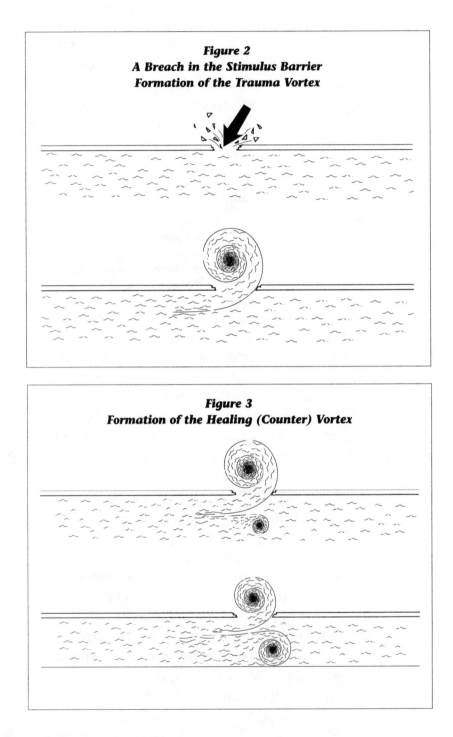

Figure 2
A Breach in the Stimulus Barrier
Formation of the Trauma Vortex

Figure 3
Formation of the Healing (Counter) Vortex

We re-enact and relive our traumas when we get sucked into the trauma vortex, thus opening the possibility for emotional flooding and re-traumatization. In avoiding the trauma vortex, we constrict and become phobic. We do not allow ourselves to experience the fullness of what we are inside, or, what there is outside. This split-off whirlpool sucks away much of our life-energy, reducing the force of the main current.

Nature responds, thank goodness, by immediately creating a counter-vortex—a healing vortex—to balance the force of the trauma vortex. This balancing force instantly begins to rotate in the opposite direction of the trauma vortex. The new whirlpool exists "within" the banks of mainstream experience (Fig. 3).

With the creation of this healing vortex, our choices are no longer limited to either reliving our traumas or avoiding them. There exists now a third option—one that I call "renegotiation." In renegotiating trauma, we begin to mend the ruptured bank by circling around the peripheries of the healing and trauma vortices, gradually moving toward their centers. We begin by riding the warble (wobbly oscillation) created by these two opposing forces, experiencing the turbulence between them. We then move slowly and rhythmically, back and forth, from one to the other in a figure-eight pattern. By beginning with the healing vortex, we pick up the support and resources needed to successfully negotiate the trauma vortex. By moving between these vortices, we release the tightly bound energies at their cores—as if they were being unwound. We move toward their centers and their energies are released; the vortices break up, dissolve, and are integrated back into the mainstream. This is renegotiation (Fig. 4).

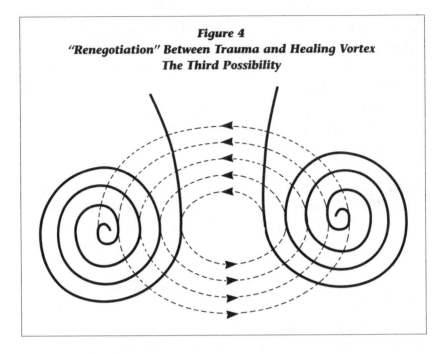

Figure 4
"Renegotiation" Between Trauma and Healing Vortex
The Third Possibility

Margaret

Margaret is a client who has a close enough natural connection with the felt sense that she does not censor or interfere with the healing process once it begins. She is a middle-aged physician who has had years of recurring symptoms such as neck pain and lower abdominal cramping, for which no cause could be found in spite of extensive testing and unsuccessful treatment.

As our session begins, Margaret tells me she feels an asymmetrical tension in her neck. I encourage her to observe that sensation. As she focuses on the tension, her head initiates a subtle turning motion (orienting response) to the left. After a few minutes, her legs begin to tremble gently (discharge). She feels pleasure in the release, but is suddenly startled by the image of a man's face. After moving through a series of uncomfortable bodily sensations and waves of emotion, other images begin to unfold: She "remembers" (at age five) being tied to a tree by a man who rips off her clothes, swats her, then pushes a stick into her vagina. Margaret again moves through a swell of emotion but remains connected with her physical sensations. Next, she is lying on a bed of raked leaves. She feels excited, yet calm.

Suddenly she sees a vivid, detailed image of the man's face. It is red and contorted. Beads of sweat drip from his forehead. Then, in the same breath, Margaret shifts again and describes the autumn leaves on the ground. They are all around her. She reports that she is frolicking in the leaves and feels a crisp sensation. She is delighted. In her next image, she is once again being tied to the tree. She sees the man with his fly open, his penis hanging out. He cuts a rabbit open with a knife and screams at her that he will kill her if she tells anyone. She has the sensation of her "head going crazy inside." Next, she is in the arms of her grandmother, telling her what happened. Tears flow from Margaret's eyes as she reports feeling deeply comforted. In the next scene, she is again rolling in the pile of leaves. She laughs and rolls from side to side with her arms wrapped around her chest. The tension Margaret experienced in her neck disappeared after this session. We worked together a few more times and she was able to eliminate the abdominal symptoms. Most important is what she described as a new symptom in her life—joy!

What Really Happened?

In Margaret's case, independent reports of the incident (including medical evidence and police involvement) substantiate the basic facts of her story. However, the startling truth is that after helping thousands of clients track their felt sense experience, I can say with no hesitation whatsoever that *whether Margaret's story was completely accurate or completely "fabricated" doesn't matter at all in terms of healing her traumatic symptoms.*

Did Margaret move through her traumatic symptoms because she returned to the past and "relived" a literal account of the experience she had as a child? Or did she have an experience as an adult in which her organism creatively brought forth fragments of several different events from disparate points in time and space to support the healing process? In order for the first explanation to be accurate, the man must have untied her, let her play for a while in the leaves, and then bound her to the tree again—twice. This is, of course, possible. But would she have really frolicked in such a situation? That does not seem likely. It is more likely that she played in leaves at a different time and brought in that image as a resource to help strengthen her healing vortex.

What about the image of the man with his penis hanging out which is followed immediately by his cutting a rabbit open and screaming at her? Does this seem to be a literal account? If so, where did the man get the rabbit? Again, it is possible that the account is an accurate report of what happened. However, several other interpretations are also possible.

The man could have told her he would cut her up like a rabbit. Or at some other time she could have been frightened by seeing, or even reading about, a rabbit being cut open. Her felt sense may have suggested the image as a metaphor for how she felt. The image does certainly convey the sense of horror a young child might have experienced in such a situation.

What really happened is that Margaret, as an adult, was able to follow the creative dictates of her organism. Her consciousness shifted between images that evoked the horror she experienced as a child (the trauma vortex) and other images that allowed her to expand and heal (the healing vortex). By staying in touch with the sensations that accompanied these images, Margaret allowed her organism to experience a rhythmic pulsation between these vortices that helped her synthesize a new reality while discharging and healing her traumatic reaction. Through the guiding languages of felt sensation, Margaret was able to renegotiate the terror that had persisted in her neck and abdomen for decades following this horrific event. The healing was orchestrated by the transformative relationship between the healing and trauma vortices.

Before learning the ways of the felt sense, most people respond to the emergence of the healing vortex and the positive sensations that come with it by squelching or ignoring them—by avoiding them. Healing images can be disconcerting when we are fixated on terrifying visions. In our zeal to recover more of the "memory" of what happened, we suppress the expansion that the nervous system so desperately seeks and plunge head on into the trauma vortex. The secret to Margaret's healing was that she did not do this. When the image of the leaves came, she went with the feelings associated with it fully and completely and moved away from the horrible feelings of being tied to the tree and terrorized. The leaves (associated with the healing vortex) allowed her to face the deepest parts of her trauma without being overwhelmed. As a result, she transformed herself into a more integrated, resourceful person.

Renegotiation and Re-enactment

*About five months before arrival at Jupiter, Galileo's
probe is to separate from the mothership. This maneuver
must aim the probe precisely since it has no navigation
or propulsion systems...As it plummets toward the planet
fast enough to go from Los Angeles to Washington in
90 seconds, a wrong entry could send it skipping off the
tip of Jupiter's atmosphere and careening into space or
burning to a cinder (if it enters Jupiter's atmosphere
too directly).*
—Science Section, International Herald Tribune
   October 12, 1989, by Kathy Sawyer

Transforming trauma isn't a mechanical ritual that traumatized people can perform and then sit back and complacently expect results. There is no magic pill. Transformation requires a willingness to challenge your basic beliefs about who you are. We must have the faith to trust responses and sensations that we can't fully understand, and a willingness to experience ourselves flowing in harmony with the primitive, natural laws that will take over and balance our seemingly incongruous perceptions. Traumatized people must let go of all kinds of beliefs and preconceptions in order to complete the journey back to health. Remember, letting go never happens all at once.

The following diagram (Fig. 5) depicts someone entering into a traumatic event (a roller coaster ride with an inverted loop of track). In re-enactment we go into the loop, and as we start to go upside down, we hold on by bracing and tightening our entire bodies. We don't know that the centrifugal law of physics will prevent us from falling and being killed or injured. When we re-enact we may experience terror and/or the exhilaration of surviving it. We may also become addicted to the relief and thrill that ensues when we confront our deepest fears. However, we will not learn the true mastery

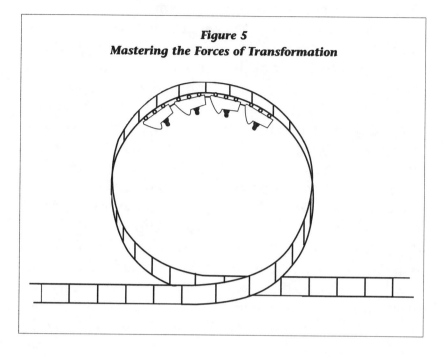

Figure 5
Mastering the Forces of Transformation

and surrender that occurs when our traumas are transformed.

In renegotiation we gradually get to understand
these laws and forces so that we can learn to trust them
and surrender to them. We can experience excitement
without becoming tense or terrified. We can acquire a
true sense of mastery.

In Somatic Experiencing, renegotiation revolves
around learning to experience the natural restorative
laws of the organism. Marius (Chapter Nine) and Margaret (this chapter) experienced their sensations in going
through the loop of the trauma and healing vortices. In
surrendering to natural laws, they gained mastery. The
forces they learned to master are centrifugal—like the
forces that are set up when moving between the healing
and trauma vortices. By moving through the warble and

entering the healing vortex, then moving rhythmically back and forth between the two, these traumatized individuals gradually became certain that they would not be sucked into a black hole and burned to a cinder, or propelled into outer space. In re-enacting their experiences, Marius and Margaret may have learned that they could survive. They would not, however, have learned the new responses that would allow them to master the powerful forces set into motion by traumatic events. When we set up our initial conditions correctly and come into alignment (like the *Galileo Probe*), we can put our trust in the natural laws to guide us on our healing journey.

One of the most profound and conceptually challenging aspects of healing trauma is understanding the role played by memory. Many of us have the faulty and limiting belief that to heal our traumas we must dredge up horrible memories from the past. What we know for certain is that we feel damaged, fragmented, distressed, shameful, unhappy, etc. In an attempt to feel better we search for the cause(s) of our unhappiness, hoping that finding them will ease our distress.

Even if we are able to dredge up reasonably accurate "memories" of an event, they will not heal us. On the contrary, this unnecessary exercise can cause us to re-enact the experience and get sucked into the trauma vortex once again. The search for memories may engender more pain and distress, while further solidifying our frozen immobility. The vicious cycle then escalates as we are compelled to search for other explanatory events ("memories") to account for our additional distress. How important are these memories?

There are two kinds of memory pertinent to trauma. One form is somewhat like a video camera, sequentially recording events. It is called "explicit" (conscious) memory, and stores information such as what you did at the party last night. The other form is the way that the human organism organizes the experience of significant events—for example, the procedure of how to ride a bicycle. This type of memory is called "implicit" (procedural) and is unconscious. It has to do with things we don't think about; our bodies just do them.

In many ways, the seemingly concrete images of a traumatized person's "memory" can be the most difficult to let go of. This is particularly true when the person has previously attempted to move through a traumatic reaction using forms of psychotherapy that encourage catharsis and the emotional reliving of the traumatic event as the panacea for recovery. Catharsis reinforces memory as an absolute truth and inadvertently reinforces the trauma vortex. An incorrect understanding of memory is one of the misconceptions that interferes with the transformation process.

What Is Memory?

The brain's function is to choose from the past, to diminish it, to simplify it, but not to preserve it.
—Henri Bergson, The Creative Mind, 1911

Bergson was years ahead of his time with his assertion that the brain's function is not to preserve the past. Many theorists tell us the idea that "you can know what happened because you remember it" is an illusion produced by a human need to create meaning out of the various elements of experience. In *The Invention of Memory*, Israel Rosenfield eloquently combs the beach of conscious experience and comes to a number of startling conclusions—particularly, that the idea of memory as we normally conceive it is both inadequate and misleading. He reasons that "it is not fixed images that we rely on, but recreations—imaginations—the past remolded in ways appropriate for the present." Gerald Edelman, who won the Nobel Prize for his earlier work in immunology, aptly calls these phenomena "The Remembered Present." Akhter Ahsen in his book *Basic Concepts in Eidetic Psychotherapy*[11] has shown that there exists an antithesis between creativity and static memory.

Rather than recording a linear sequence of events, memory is more like playing with Mr. Potato Head. Depending on how it feels at the time, the mind selects from colors, images, sounds, smells, interpretations, and responses with similar arousal and feeling tones, then brings them to the foreground in various combinations to produce what we call memory. As it relates to survival, memory is a particular type of perception; it is not an accurate imprint of an event. In this sense, it is the process by which the organism creates a gestalt (functional unit) of the experience. This gestalt can be a faithful representation of an actual event or it can just as easily be a rendering consisting of unrelated data from several different events—in other words, a mosaic. This is why eye-witnesses often give surprisingly different descriptions of the same incident.

Brain and Memory

For more than a hundred years scientists have been demonstrating that the brain is divided into areas specifically responsible for different senses. There are centers for vision, hearing, smell, taste, skin sensation, etc. A prevailing supposition used to be that there must also be specific areas of the brain where memories are recorded as complete imprints of events that an individual has experienced. Let's review the results of a couple

---

[11] Brandon House, 1968

of experiments that supported or challenged the validity of this theory.

Penfield's experiments on epileptic patients. Much of the popular belief that we have fixed memory traces in our brains was deeply influenced by the work of the eminent Canadian neurosurgeon, Wilder Penfield. In classic experiments done in the 1930s (reported in *Mysteries of the Mind*)[12] Penfield used small point stimulation of electricity to probe the brains of hundreds of conscious adults who suffered from epilepsy. He wanted to know if there were regions of the brain that could be surgically removed (if they were not involved in a vital function) in order to eliminate epileptic seizures. Penfield reported that: *Suddenly [his patient] is aware of all that was in his mind during an earlier strip of time. It is the stream of a former consciousness (a memory) flowing again...Sometimes he is aware of all that he was seeing at the moment...It stops when the electrode is lifted...This electrical recall is completely at random...most often the event was neither significant nor important.* Penfield (and those who followed in his footsteps) concluded that he had discovered the existence of permanent memories etched in specific areas of the brain. Until recently other scientists concurred. However, Penfield's own notes make it clear that most of these "flashbacks" were more like dreams than memories. The patients often said things like "I keep having dreams...I keep seeing things...dreaming of things." In addition, of the five-hundred-plus patients that Penfield studied, only forty (less than eight percent) reported having recall experiences of any kind.

Lashley's experiments with rats. Independently, around the time of Penfield's surgical observations, experimental psychologist Karl Lashley was also attempting to discov-

---

[12] Princeton University Press, 1975

er the areas of the brain that carried the imprint of memory. Lashley performed an extensive series of rather grisly experiments in which he taught rats to find their way through a maze and then systematically chopped up parts of their brains. Even after their cerebral cortices had been all but destroyed, the rats could still find their way through the maze. To Lashley's amazement, their memory of the maze remained in place up until the point that the rats had too little brain left to do much of anything. Lashley spent almost thirty years of his life searching for the location of memory in the brain. He never found it.

In spite of the expenditure of hundreds of millions of dollars and the efforts of some of science's brightest minds, little evidence has ever been found of a complete memory that has its own location in the brain. This surprising revelation has prompted speculation and conjecture regarding the nature of memory. The groundbreaking work led by Edelman, Rosenfield, Ahsen and others has given us another way to look at memory. The idea that memory is not an accurate recording device turns our conventional notions upside down and backwards. In so doing, it offers a reprieve to traumatized people who are caught on the endless treadmill of trying to piece together a coherent movie of what happened to them.

But It Seems So Real!

If memories are not literal records of events, then why do some of the images created during periods of intense arousal seem so real? Recent research suggests that the realness of an image is reinforced by the intensity of the arousal associated with it. Pierre Gloor, a Montreal surgeon working in the same city as Penfield some fifty years later, discovered that the "memories" Penfield reported were only activated when the electrodes stimulated both the sensory areas and the limbic portion of the brain simultaneously. The limbic area of the brain is largely responsible for feelings and emotions. Gloor and his colleagues concluded that "some affective (emotional) or motivational significance to a perception may be…the precondition for the perception to be consciously experienced or recalled and may imply that all consciously perceived events must assume some kind of affective dimension, if ever so slight." In other words, they concluded that emotional feelings are essential for the experience of remembering.

In another study, William Gray found that juvenile offenders (to whom he was trying to teach new behaviors) only made real changes when there was an emotional tone associated with their perceptions. Otherwise, they would "forget" what they had learned. Other researchers have expanded on Gloor's and Gray's findings and their conclusions are virtually the same. An associated emotion or feeling is an essential prerequisite for any remembered element of experience. But what happens when there's an overwhelming arousal?

Life-threatening events stimulate arousal. In response, the nervous system goes into survival mode and the organism has to make an instantaneous decision. To accomplish this task, it weighs the elements of the present situation and shifts into a research mode. It compares the present to the past, looking for a response that might help resolve the current dilemma. Recorded memory would be of no use to us at this point because we have no time to run through a list. We need to have the whole picture immediately.

These pictures are organized by their levels of arousal, activation, emotion, and response. Our gestalts of experience are categorized by the levels of activation at which they occurred. An analogy of this could be a multi-storied library with several floors of shelved books. The lower stories hold books associated with lower levels of activation (arousal) and those in higher stories are related to higher levels. If we think of the books as containing images and responses (related pictures) to that level or category of activation, then at each level there are possible, appropriate resources and responses from which we can choose. When we need a response we do not search the entire library; we scan the books at the appropriate level of activation.

For example, in an ideal adaptive response to a life-threatening event, the nervous system searches for related significant images and possible responses at an appropriate level of activation and context. It then makes a selection and acts accordingly. It searches, selects, then acts. This threat-arousal sequence has to include an active response or it becomes frozen and doesn't complete.

A maladaptive response to a life-threatening event never completes itself. An example of this is when the nervous system unceasingly and unsuccessfully searches for appropriate responses. As it fails to find this critical information, the emotions of rage, terror, and helplessness escalate. This escalation spurs further activation and compels the search for significant images. Since the images it finds are associated with traumatic emotions, the images themselves may evoke further activation without supplying the appropriate response to complete the process. In turn, further escalated arousal provokes a more frantic search for any significant image. The result is a continuing and ever-escalating spiral in which we search for images stored on our bookshelves. As our emotions escalate, we become more desperate to find the appropriate response to our situation and begin to indiscriminately select any image or "memory." All of the images selected are related to highly aroused, similar emotional states, but are not necessarily useful to our survival at that moment. They are the fuel of the "trauma vortex."

Any emotional activation coupled with an image generates an experience of memory. When a person, in desperation, selects images associated with a similar emotional tone even though they may be dissimilar in content, a "memory" is created. This memory is often accepted as the absolute truth of what happened. Because of the high level of emotion attached to this experience, the traumatized person believes it to be truth. What if a person reaches this high emotional level during a therapy session? Any suggestion or leading question by the therapist will almost certainly be incorporated into this escalating, narrowing version of an experience. The person will begin to accept this version as the absolute truth, and will tenaciously cling to that emotional truth. Memories need to be understood, both from relative and absolute perspectives.

When we don't become invested in finding a literal truth, we remain free to experience the full and compassionate healing afforded by the rhythmic exchange between the trauma and healing vortices that occur in renegotiation. When we allow ourselves to create a "memory" that is not necessarily literal, as did Margaret, Marius and many others, we give ourselves permission to heal. While we don't have a literal, emotionally bound conviction of "the truth," we do gain a compassionate perspective for our own vitality, strength and resourcefulness. Often, we get a sense of what may have happened to us in the past. It is prudent that we hold our "memories" in perspective, and not feel compelled to accept them as the literal truth. We can accept these historical ambiguities as a melding of experiences.

Remember, most memory is not a coherent and continuous record of something that actually happened. It is a process of assembling elements of our experience into a coherent, organized whole. In addition, we often separate the elements of a traumatizing experience into fragments in order to de-intensify the emotions and sensations. Consequently, only fragments of a remembered traumatic event are likely to be entirely accurate. In general, a complete "memory" of a traumatic experience is much more likely to be a compilation of elements from a variety of experiences. The elements that are drawn to this "melting pot" can originate in the actual experiences that people have had, and/or in experiences they had while reading books or newspapers, hearing stories, dreaming, watching a movie, talking with a friend (or a therapist), etc. In short, any type of sensory or informational input that has a similar emotional or feeling tone may be summoned to produce "the memory." As far as the organism is concerned, all these elements of experience are equivalent if they carry a similar type of arousal and emotional impact.

What the felt sense is trying to communicate is "This is how I feel." However, because the state of arousal activates an intense searching response, the person experiencing the arousal is predisposed (correctly or incorrectly) to interpret any such information as the "cause" of the activation—in other words, as the actual memory of the event. Because the emotions that accompany trauma are so intense, the so-called memory can seem more real than life itself. In addition, if there are pressures from group members or therapists, books, or other mass media, individuals experiencing emotional distress search for the cause of their distress and are susceptible to these types of invented memories. This is how so-called false memories can be produced.

Unfortunately, many therapists employ intense emotional release techniques to work with traumatic (or other) symptoms. It is just this type of emotional push-ing that can activate states of high arousal. When this happens, we see the appearance of powerful experien-tial collages that are perceived (to the degree of their intensity) to be "true" memories. It is not important whether memories are objectively accurate. Of prime importance is whether the associated activation esca-lates or resolves. It is essential that the unresolved acti-vation locked in the nervous system be discharged. This transformation has nothing to do with memory. It has to do with the process of completing our survival instincts.

Some people find it difficult to accept the idea that memory isn't a continuous record of reality. It is a dis-concerting thought. The memories we have about where we have been and what we have done contribute great-ly to our conscious and unconscious ideas about who we are. Memories are regarded by many as a treasured pos-session, even if they are not consciously recognized as a basis for one's very identity.

When we perceive memory as a "mixed bag" of information, images, and responses, we open the door to freedom. A fixed memory of literally recorded events often limits and confines us. In a sense, when we cling strongly to the concrete version of memory we are re-stricted to doing what we have always done in relation to it. The dilemma is that unresolved trauma forces us to repeat what we have done before. New and creative assemblages of possibilities will not easily occur to us. The key to transforming trauma is to move slowly in the direction of flexibility and spontaneity.

When we are traumatized, there is an eventual disruption in the way that we process information. The organism becomes disorganized and loses much of its fluidity and normal capacity to categorize information. The normal, self-organizing function of the organism has to be re-established. If we feel inclined to focus on memories (even if they are basically accurate), it is important to understand that this choice will impair our ability to move out of our traumatic reactions. Transformation requires change. One of the things that must change is the relationship that we have with our "memories."

But I'm Proud to Be a Survivor

There ain't no future in the past
—Country-western song

We trauma sufferers search for memories of abuse in order to explain our feelings of victimization and help-lessness. We also need to take pride in ourselves as survivors. Being able to recall a terrible scenario and to know that you have survived it is an important element in building self-esteem. Important as that element is, it pales beside the healthy sense of resolution, mastery, and empowerment that accompanies true healing and transformation. "Survivor's pride" is an indication that healthy functioning is trying to assert itself. Knowing that you have survived feels good because it enables the constricted (traumatized) sense of self to enjoy some empowerment and expansion. It can provide us with a source of identity. It hints at completion, and is a good place to begin the healing journey.

Giving up the idea that memories are concrete and accurate representations of actual past events doesn't mean foregoing the experience of expansion and affirmation of life that comes with traveling the survivor route. One of my clients, while working through his childhood abuse at the hands of "barrio" gang members, said it this way: "I don't have to justify my experience with memories any more."

Feelings of pleasure and expansion are evidence that the organism is moving into the healing vortex. The key to letting the healing vortex support the process of transformation lies in the ability to let go of preconceived ideas about how an event "should be" remembered. In other words, you have to be able to give the felt sense free license to communicate without censoring what it has to say. Paradoxically, this doesn't negate the liberating significance of acknowledging "what really happened." This truth is experienced in moving fluidly between the healing and trauma vortices. There is a deep acceptance of the emotional impact of events in our lives along with a simultaneous quality of *waking up* from a nightmare. One awakens from this dream with a sense of wonder and gladness.

The Courage to Feel

If you want to know whether an event "really" happened, all I can do is wish you well and tell you what you already know. You may have taken on an impossible task. In my view, neither this book nor anything else will help you know the truth of what you are seeking. If, on the other hand, your primary goal is to heal, there is much here that can help you.

If healing is what you want, your first step is to be open to the possibility that literal truth is not the most important consideration. The conviction that it really happened, the fear that it may have happened, the subtle searching for evidence that it did happen, can all get in your way as you try to hear what the felt sense wants to tell you about what it needs to heal.

By committing yourself to the process of healing, you will come to learn more about the truth behind your reactions. In spite of the fragmentation that occurs in the wake of trauma, the organism does retain associations that are connected with the events that caused its debilitation. The felt sense may reveal these events to you, or it may not. Keep reminding yourself that it doesn't matter. Because if healing is what you want, it doesn't matter whether you know the concrete truth.

Desire and Healing

The process of healing begins from within. Even before the cast is set on our broken bones, our bones begin to knit themselves back together. Just as there are physical laws that affect the healing of our bodies, there are laws that affect the healing of our minds. We have seen how our intellects can override some powerful instinctual forces of our organisms.

Sometimes, traumatized individuals have an investment in being ill and may form a kind of attachment to their symptoms. There are innumerable reasons (both physiological and psychological) to explain why this attachment occurs. I don't think it's necessary to go into detail on this subject. The important thing to keep in mind is that we can only heal to the degree that we can become unattached from these symptoms. It is almost as if they become entities unto themselves through the power we give them. We need to release them from our minds and hearts along with the energy that is locked in our nervous systems.

With a Little Help From Our Friends

Once an affliction of the mind has been conquered,
it cannot return.
—Thrangu Rimpoche

I must confess that the miracles of healing I have seen make some higher form of wisdom and order hard to deny. Perhaps a better way of putting it is that there is an innate natural wisdom whose laws provide order in the universe. It is certainly far more powerful than any individual's personal history. The organism, subject to these laws, tracks its way through even the most horrific experiences imaginable. How can such a thing happen if there is no god, no wisdom, no tiger in the universe?

People who have worked through traumatic reactions frequently tell me that there is both an animalistic and a spiritual dimension to their lives afterwards. They are more spontaneous and less inhibited in the expression of healthy assertion and joy. They more readily identify themselves with the experience of being an animal. At the same time, they perceive themselves as having become more human. When trauma is transformed, one of the gifts of healing is a childlike awe and reverence for life.

When we are overwhelmed by trauma (and then rebound), we become awed by the natural laws in force. In losing our innocence, we can gain wisdom, and in the process of gaining wisdom, we gain a new innocence. The instinctual organism does not sit in judgment; it only does what it does. All you have to do is get out of the way.

In renegotiating trauma by moving between the trauma and healing vortices, we engage the universal law of polarity. This law is available to us as a tool to help us transform our traumas. In this process we are also directly experiencing the rhythmic pulsing of life. Through the utilization of universal laws, we begin to recognize the cyclic patterns from which our reality is woven. Ultimately, this can lead to a higher understanding of the relationship between life and death.

...despite our differences, we're all alike. Beyond
identities and desires, there is a common core of self -
an essential humanity whose nature is peace and whose
expression is thought and whose action is unconditional
love. When we identify with that inner core, respecting
and honoring it in others as well as ourselves, we
experience healing in every area of life."
—Joan Borysenko, *Minding the Body, Mending the Mind*

15
The Eleventh Hour:
Transforming Societal Trauma

Technology and rapid population growth are bringing us
into a world where time and distance do little to separate
us. At the same time, we face serious threats to ourselves
and our planet. We live with war, terrorism, the possibility of annihilation from "super weapons", a growing
split between haves and have-nots, and environmental
destruction. Citizens in our inner cities randomly destroy
property and life as the effects of years of accumulated
stress, trauma, hostility, and economic oppression com-
bust. The rich swallow up each other's companies in
primitive, ritualistic feeding frenzies. The outlook
becomes even more grim when we consider the frightening potential for violence in a soon-to-be mature gener-
ation of children born with drug addictions.

As the world population increases and our communities become more interconnected, it becomes imperative that we learn to live and work together in harmony.
We have problems that will destroy us if we cannot work
together effectively to solve them. Yet, rather than negotiate economic, ethnic, and geographical issues, individ-

221

uals and communities seem bent on destroying one another. It is to these issues that the causes of war are often ascribed. But are they the root causes? Our survival as a species and the survival of this planet may lie in our ability to answer this question.

The roots of war run deep. Any truly honest person will acknowledge that we all have the capacity for both violence and love. Both are equally basic aspects of the human experience. What may be even more significant in understanding the roots of war is the human vulnerability to traumatization. We should not forget that it was in the frightening symptoms manifested by some of the soldiers who returned from combat that the effects of trauma were first recognized. As we discussed in the last chapter, trauma creates a compelling drive for re-enactment when we are unaware of its impact upon us.

What if entire communities of people are driven into mass re-enactments by experiences such as war? In the face of such mass mindless compulsion, a "New World Order" would become a meaningless polemic. Lasting peace among warring peoples cannot be accomplished without first healing the traumas of previous terrorism, violence, and horror on a mass scale. Does the drive for re-enactment propel societies who have a history of waging war on one another into confrontation after confrontation? Consider the evidence and decide for yourself.

The Animal Approach to Aggression

Most animals in the course of feeding or mating exhibit aggressive behaviors. Thanks to National Geographic and other programs about wildlife, these behaviors are well known to us. Animals routinely kill and eat members of *other* species. When it comes to members of their own species, Nature seems to have drawn a line that animals rarely cross. There are some exceptions, but generally speaking, members of the same species rarely kill or even seriously injure one another. In spite of the strong evolutionary imperative that drives animal aggression, most wild creatures have taboos about killing their own kind.

Within species, there have evolved ritualized behaviors that usually prevent mortal injury. Animals of the same species exhibit these behaviors both for the act of aggression itself as well as to signal that the confrontation is over. For instance, when male deer confront one another, they use their antlers to "lock heads." The purpose of the encounter is not to kill the other deer but rather to establish dominance. The ensuing struggle is clearly more like a wrestling match than a duel to the death. When one of the deer establishes its superiority, the other leaves the area and the matter is finished. If, on the other hand, the deer is attacked by a member of another species such as a mountain lion, it will use those antlers to gore its attacker.

Similarly, when fighting with members of their own species, most dogs and wolves bite to wound, not to kill. In other species a display of color, plumage, dance, or threatening behavior determines which aggressor will emerge the victor. Even animals that have evolved a particularly lethal means of defending themselves typically do not use this advantage against members of their own species. Piranhas fight one another by lashing out with their tails; rattlesnakes butt heads until one of them collapses.

Ritualistic behaviors also frequently signal the close of an aggressive encounter between members of the same species. A confrontation between two animals typically ends with some form of submissive posturing (e.g., when a weaker animal rolls onto its back and makes itself completely vulnerable by exposing its belly to the victor). Within species, these gestures, like the various forms of ritualized combat, are universally recognized and respected. This is remarkable in light of the fact that members of the same species share identical requirements for food, shelter, and mating. Nonetheless, there is a clear evolutionary advantage. In helping to define orderly social and reproductive hierarchies, these behaviors promote the overall well-being of the group as well as enhance the ultimate survival of the species.

Human Aggression

In the days of the hunter-gatherer, fighting was apparently limited by the same sorts of inhibiting behaviors that work effectively for animal species. Obviously this is not the case for modern "civilized" humans. Being human, we recognize the evolutionary prohibition against killing members of the same species in the same way that animals do. Generally, there are rules or laws that exact some form of punishment for killing a member of one's own community, but these laws don't apply to the killing that takes place in war.

When we look more closely at the anthropology of human warfare, we do not find killing and maiming the enemy to be a universal objective. Among some groups, at least, we find evidence of a reticence to engage in violence and brutality on a large scale. Some peoples use ritualistic behaviors quite reminiscent of the animal manner of dealing with aggression. Among Eskimo cultures, aggression between tribes or neighboring communities is unheard of. Within these communities, conflict between opponents may be settled by wrestling, cuffing ears, or butting heads. Eskimos are also known to settle conflicts through singing duels in which songs are composed to fit the occasion and the winner is determined by an audience. Some "primitive" cultures terminate their skirmishes when one of the tribal members is injured or killed.

These are a few examples of human ritual behavior whose purpose is to maintain the taboo against killing within the species. At the biological level, we find a creature more easily distinguished from other animals by its intelligence rather than by its teeth, venom, claws, or strength. Is intelligence an attribute intended to be used in service of torture, rape, death, and violence? If you listen to the news, it might lead you to think so.

Why Do Humans Kill, Maim, and Torture One Another?

Even when competing for their most basic resources-food and territory-animals typically do not kill members of their own species. Why do we? What has happened to propagate large-scale killing and violence as human populations increase in number and complexity? While there are many theories of war, there is one root cause that seems not to have been widely acknowledged.

Trauma is among the most important root causes for the form modern warfare has taken. The perpetuation, escalation, and violence of war can be attributed in part to post-traumatic stress. Our past encounters with one another have generated a legacy of fear, separation, prejudice, and hostility. This legacy is a legacy of trauma fundamentally no different from that experienced by individuals—except in its scale.

Traumatic re-enactment is one of the strongest and most enduring reactions that occurs in the wake of trauma. Once we are traumatized, it is almost certain that we will continue to repeat or re-enact parts of the experience in some way. We will be drawn over and over again into situations that are reminiscent of the original trauma. When people are traumatized by war, the implications are staggering.

Let's review what we know about trauma. When people are traumatized, our internal systems remain aroused. We become hypervigilant but are unable to locate the source of this pervasive threat. This situation causes fear and reactivity to escalate, amplifying the need to identify the source of the threat. The result: we become likely candidates for re-enactment—in search of an enemy.

Imagine now an entire population of people with a similar post-traumatic history. Now, imagine two such populations located in the same geographical region, perhaps with different languages, colors, religions, or ethnic traditions. The consequences are inevitable. The disturbing arousal with its ongoing perception of danger is now "explained." The threat has been located: it is them. They are enemy. The urge to kill, maim, and mutilate escalates—these two "neighbors" seem compelled to slaughter each other. They destroy each other's homes, hopes, and dreams. By doing so, they kill their own futures.

While war is complex and can hardly be attributed to a single cause, nations living in close proximity do have a disturbing tendency to make war on one another. This is a pattern that has played and replayed innumerable times in recorded history. Trauma has a frightening potential to be re-enacted in the form of violence. The Serbs, Moslems, and Croats have been repeating their violence as virtual instant replays of World Wars One and Two, and perhaps as far back as the Ottoman Empire. Middle Eastern nations can trace their replays to Biblical times. In places where actual wars do not repeat with the kind of ferocity and brutality that is seen regularly around the globe, other forms of violence prevail. Murder, poverty, homelessness, child abuse, racial and religious hatred and persecution are all related to war. There is no avoiding the traumatic aftermath of war; it reaches into every segment of a society.

Circle of Trauma, Circle of Grace

Healthy babies are born with a complex array of behaviors, feelings, and perceptions. These elements are designed to facilitate exploration and bonding and eventually healthy social behaviors. When infants are born into a life of stress and trauma, these life-promoting behaviors are interfered with. Instead of exploration and bonding, these babies are inhibited and exhibit fearful and withdrawn behaviors. As young children and adults, they will be less social and more inclined to violence. Healthy exploration and bonding seem to be antidotes that mitigate against violence and disorder.

Transforming Cultural Trauma

Just as the effects of individual trauma can be transformed, the aftereffects of war on a societal level can also be resolved. People can and must come together with a willingness to share rather than to fight, to transform trauma rather than to propagate it. A place to begin is with our children. They can provide the bridge that enables all of us to experience closeness and bonding with those we may formerly have regarded with animosity.

Several years ago, Dr. James Prescott (then with the National Institute of Mental Health), presented important anthropological research on the effect of infant and child-rearing practices on violent behavior in aboriginal societies[13]. He reported that the societies that practiced close physical bonding and the use of stimulating rhythmical movement had a low incidence of violence. Societies with diminished or punitive physical contact with their children showed clear tendencies toward violence in the forms of war, rape, and torture.

The work of Dr. Prescott (and others), points to something we all know intuitively: that the time around birth and infancy is a critical period. Children assimilate the ways that their parents relate to each other and the world at a very young age When parents have been traumatized, they have difficulty teaching their young a sense of basic trust. Without this sense of trust as a resource, children are more vulnerable to trauma. One solution to breaking the cycle of trauma is to involve infants and mothers in an experience that generates trust and bonding before the child has completely absorbed the parents' distrust of themselves and others.

In Norway, exciting work is now being done in this area. My colleague, Eldbjörg Wedaa, and I are using what we know about this critical period of infancy. This approach allows an entire group of people to begin transforming the traumatic remnants of previous encounters. This method requires a room, a few simple musical instruments, and blankets that are strong enough to hold a baby's weight.

The process works as follows: a group composed of mothers and infants from opposing factions (religious, racial, political, etc.) is brought together at a home or a community center. The encounter begins with this mixed group of mothers and infants taking turns teaching one another simple folk songs from their respective cultures. Holding their babies, the mothers rock and dance while they sing the songs to their children. A facilitator uses

---

[13] Body, Pleasure, and the Origins of Violence—Futurist Magazine, April/May, 1975—Atomic Scientist, November, 1975

simple instruments to enhance the rhythm in the songs. The movement, rhythm, and singing strengthen the neurological patterns that produce peaceful alertness and receptivity. As a result, the hostility produced by generations of strife begins to soften.

At first, the children are perplexed by these goings-on, but soon they become more interested and involved. They are enthusiastic about the rattles, drums, and tambourines that the facilitator passes to them. Characteristically, without rhythmical stimulation, children of this age will do little more than try to fit objects such as these into their mouths. Here, however, the children will join in generating the rhythm with great delight, often squealing and cooing with glee.

Because infants are highly developed organisms at birth, they send signals that activate their mother's deepest sense of serenity, responsiveness, and biological competence. In this healthy relationship, the mothers and their young feed off each other in an exchange of mutually gratifying physiological responses, which in turn generate feelings of security and pleasure. It is here that the cycle of traumatic damage begins to transform.

The transformation continues as the mothers place their babies on the floor and allow them to explore. Like luminous magnets, the babies joyfully move toward each other, overcoming barriers of shyness as the mothers quietly support their exploration by forming a circle around them. The sense of mutual connection that is generated by this small adventure is difficult to describe or imagine—it must be witnessed.

The large group then breaks up into smaller groups, each consisting of a mother and infant from each culture. The two mothers swing their infants gently in a blanket. These babies aren't just happy, they are completely "blissed out". They generate a roomful of love that is so contagious that soon the mothers (and fathers when culturally appropriate) are smiling at each other and enjoying an experience of deep bonding with members of a community that earlier they feared and distrusted. The mothers leave with renewed hearts and spirits and are eager to share this feeling with others. The process is almost self-replicating.

The beauty of this approach to community healing lies in its simplicity and its effectiveness. An outside facilitator begins the process by leading the first group. After that, some of the mothers who have participated can be trained as facilitators for other groups. The primary attributes required by a facilitator are an acute sensitivity to timing and to interpersonal boundaries. It is our experience that for certain individuals, these are skills that can be easily learned through a combination of participatory experience and explanation. Once trained, the mothers become ambassadors of peace within their own communities.

"Give me a place to put my lever," exclaimed Archimedes, "and I will move the world." In a world of conflict, destruction, and trauma, we find one such fulcrum in the close physical, rhythmic pulsation between mother and infant. Experiences such as the one just described can bring people together so that they can again begin to live in harmony. Trauma's impact is different for each of us. We must all be willing to accept the responsibility for our own healing. If we continue to wage war on each other, the healing most of us yearn for will be no more than a dream.

Nations living near each other can break the generational cycle of destruction, violence, and repeated trauma that holds them hostage. By using the human organism's capacity to register peaceful aliveness, even in the web of traumatic defensiveness, we can all begin to make our communities safe for ourselves and our children. Once we establish safe communities, we can begin the process of healing ourselves and our world.

Epilogue or Epitaph?

An Armenian villager laments, "It will be a hundred years before I can talk to my neighbor again." In America's inner cities, pressures rise to the brink of destructive chaos and then crash into it. In Northern Ireland, people separated only by clotheslines and different religions watch their children waging war on each other rather than playing together.

Untraumatized humans prefer to live in harmony if they can. Yet traumatic residue creates a belief that we are unable to surmount our hostility, and that misunderstandings will always keep us apart. The experience of bonding described earlier is only one example of the many concepts and practices that could be used to address this most serious dilemma. As time and money become available, we can develop other ways to bring pregnant women, older children, and fathers into the circle of peaceful co-existence.

These approaches are not panaceas, but they are a place to begin. They offer hope where political solutions alone have not worked. The holocaust, conflicts in Iraq and Yugoslavia, the riots in Detroit, Los Angeles, and other cities—all of these encounters have been traumatic for the world community. They portray, too graphically, the price we will pay as a society if we leave the cycle of trauma intact. We must be passionate in our search for effective avenues of resolution. The survival of our species may depend on it.

Nature Is No Fool

Trauma cannot be ignored. It is an inherent part of the primitive biology that brought us here. The only way we will be able to release ourselves, individually and collectively, from re-enacting our traumatic legacies is by transforming them through renegotiation. Whether we choose to transform these legacies through group experiences, shamanic practices, or individually, it must be done.

IV
First Aid

16

Administering (Emotional) First Aid After an Accident

This chapter provides a step-by-step procedure for working with an adult. Here is a basic example of what happens at the time of an accident and how you can help prevent long-term trauma from developing. Always use your own best judgment to assess the particular circumstances you may be dealing with. What is given here are simply some guidelines.

Phase I: Immediate Action (at the scene of the accident)

- If life-saving medical procedures are required, of course that must take precedence.
- Keep the person warm, lying down, and still—unless, of course, they face further danger remaining where they are.
- Don't let them jump up, which they may be tempted to do. The feeling of having to do something, to act in some way, can override the essential need for stillness and the discharge of energy. They may want to deny the magnitude of the

accident and might act like they are fine.
- Stay with the injured person.
- Assure them that you will stay with them, that help is on the way (if it seems to be the case). They have been injured, but they are going to be OK. (obviously you need to use your judgment here-you may not want to say this if they are seriously injured.)
- Keep them warm, e.g., covered with a light blanket.
- If the accident is not too serious, encourage the person to experience their bodily sensations, which may include: "adrenaline rush", numbness, shaking and trembling, feeling hot or chilled.
- Stay present so you can help the person discharge.
- Let them know it is not only OK that they shake, but it is good and will help them release the shock. They will get a sense of relief after the shaking is completed and may feel warmth in their hands and feet. Their breathing should be fuller and easier.
- This initial phase could easily take 15-20 minutes.
- When help does arrive, continue to stay with the injured person if possible.
- If necessary, get someone to help you process the event.

Phase II: Once the Person is Moved Home or to the Hospital

- Continue to keep them quiet and resting until they are out of the acute shock reaction.
- Injured people should always take a day or two off work to allow themselves to re-integrate. This is important even if they perceive the injury

doesn't justify staying home. (This resistance can be a common denial mechanism and defense from feelings of helplessness.) Common injuries, such as whiplash, will compound and require *much* longer healing times if this initial recovery phase is bypassed. A day or two of rest is good insurance.

- In this secondary phase, the accident survivor is likely to begin to have emotions come up. Allow the emotions to be felt without judgment. They might include: anger, fear, grief, guilt, anxiety.
- The injured person may continue to have bodily sensations like shaking, chills, etc. This is still fine.

Phase III: Beginning to Access and Renegotiate the Trauma

This phase often coincides with Phase II and is essential for accessing the stored energy of trauma so that it can be fully released.

Akhter Ahsen has studied the details of what happens to a person before, during, and after a traumatic event. It is important to help people recall the peripheral images, feelings, and sensations they experienced, not just those directly related to the event.

- Throughout any of these phases, be aware that as people talk about their experiences they may become activated or agitated. Their breathing may change and become more rapid. Their heart rate might increase, or they might break into a sweat. If this happens stop talking about the experience and focus on what *sensations* they are having in their body, such as "I have a pain in my neck," or "I feel sick to my stomach."
- If you are not sure, ask them what they are feeling.

- When the people appear calmed and relaxed, move into a more detailed account of the experience and the sensations. They may notice some slight shaking and trembling. Assure them that this is natural. Point out that the activation response is decreasing and that you are working slowly to bring the energy up and discharge it. This process is known as titration (taking one small step at a time).

Following are examples of what might be experienced in each part of this process and the order in which to move through the steps.

Before the Event Occurred:
- Action—I left the house and got in the car.
- Sensations—I can feel my arms turning the wheel and my head turning to look behind me.
- Feelings—I am feeling upset.
- Image—I am driving down the highway and I notice an exit.
- Thought—I could have taken it, but I didn't. (Encourage the person to make the turn, or take that exit. It will help them reorganize the experience and release the trauma, even though the accident did occur).
- Allow time for the body discharge to occur.

After the Event:

Now, move into the details of what happened after the event.
- Image or Recollection—I am in the emergency room. The doctors are talking about me, saying, "This guy's a mess–not another one."
- Feeling—I feel guilty.
- Thought—If I had been paying attention, I could have avoided it.
- If people become activated, return to the present by focusing on bodily sensations until the energy

is discharged. After this occurs, you can gently lead them back to the details of what happened. As I mentioned before, after the trembling and discharge occur, the person will have a sense of relief, warmth in the extremities, and the ability to breathe more fully.

Just Before the Event:

Once you have successfully moved through the details before and after the accident, go to the feelings, sensations, and images related to the first recognition of impending peril. It might look something like this:

- Image—I remember seeing a yellow fender coming very close to the left side of the car. I could also see that there was a stop sign, but that the car hadn't stopped.
- Feeling—I was angry that the driver wasn't paying attention.
- Sensation—I felt my back tense as I gripped the steering wheel.
- Thought—There may be a sudden recognition, "Oh my God, it's going to happen…I'm going to die!"

You may notice that as the discharge occurs, images of the event may change.

Phase IV: Experiencing the Moment of Impact

As people re-access the moment of impact, they may hear glass shattering, the sounds of metal, or see their bodies twisting or being thrown. Explore anything (and everything) that is there through the felt sense. As reactions come up, the body may spontaneously (usually slightly) begin to move. Allow fifteen to twenty minutes for the movements to complete, facilitating the discharge of energy by focusing on the sensations in the body. After the discharge, people experience a sense of relief, usually followed by feelings of warmth in the extremities.

People may feel their bodies going rapidly in two directions, e.g., "As I was hurled into the windshield I felt my back muscles tense and pull me in the opposite direction." Reassure them that they are OK and allow them to sequence through the movements *slowly*. Some people may now re-experience a few of the more acute shock reactions such as shaking and trembling. Be supportive and acknowledge that they are making progress.

People may also experience themselves avoiding the accident completely. Or, they may jump around between the different phases outlined here. This is fine as long as they aren't entirely avoiding certain aspects, particularly the moment of impact.

It is important to stay with this phase until you can conclude at a point where the people feel a full sense of relief. Their breathing will become easier and their heart rate more steady. Achieving this goal could take as long as an hour. You can pick up where you left off and continue the process over a period of two to three days if needed. This is preferable to pushing too hard to complete it in one session. You may need to bring them back, gradually, to incomplete areas a few times to allow for full completion.

To End

After reaching the point where all phases have been satisfactorily completed, describe the entire experience again and look for activation. If the person is feeling discomfort, something may have been missed, or it may be resolved with this final review of the whole process. Suspend work unless symptoms continue or develop later. If so, review any necessary steps.

Feelings or remembrances of other experiences may also begin to come up. If this is the case, you can begin the same process we have just gone through to handle other unresolved or unrelated trauma. However, this process can take place much more slowly and over a longer period of time. If someone has a pattern or tendency for accidents, this can help prevent future incidents by reestablishing the person's innate resiliency and capacity to orient and respond.

Scenario of Healing Following an Accident

I was driving along when a car, having failed to heed the stop sign, suddenly entered the road from an intersecting side street. The other driver didn't see me in time and crashed into the left side of my car. I also didn't see him until the last minute and couldn't respond to avoid the accident.

I sat in the car for a moment, stunned. Realizing that I was OK, I got out of the car to assess the damage. Although the car was pretty badly crunched, I was not overly upset about it, because the guy had insurance and the police report would show that he was at fault. I also noticed myself thinking that I wanted to get the car repainted anyway. I felt pretty good, almost euphoric. I was pleased at how easily I moved from the accident into a difficult business meeting later that day. I was prepared for the meeting and handled it quite well. The next day I began to feel agitated. There was a stiffness in my neck, right shoulder, and arm that surprised me, since I had been hit on the left side.

Looking back at what happened earlier the day of the accident (periphery of the event), and working through the event with his friend Tom, Joe (we will call the man who had the accident Joe) remembered getting into his car to go to work and being mad at his wife.

As he recalls this, he becomes aware that his jaw is clenched and trembling. His body begins to shake and feels like it is going out of control. His friend Tom reassures him it's going to be OK. Once Joe stops shaking and feels some relief, they go on to explore more of the details prior to the accident.

Joe remembers backing out of the driveway and turning his head to the right to see where he is going. He feels his arms turning the wheel, and at the same time he notices that as a result of being angry, he is accelerating too hard. His right leg tenses as he moves his foot to the brake to slow down (he senses this action in the muscles of his legs). Encouraged by his friend Tom, Joe takes time to feel the tensing and relaxing that is happening in his right leg. As he moves from gas to brake and back again, he feels some trembling in his legs.

Then Joe remembers driving down the street and feeling that he wanted to go back to talk to his wife. With Tom's encouragement, he imagines himself turning to go back and gets a pain in his right arm that is intensifying. As they focus on that sensation, the pain begins to subside. They focus on Joe's desire to turn around. This time Joe is able to complete the turn in his body and mind and imagines returning home to resolve things with his wife. He tells her that he felt hurt at the party the night before, because she seemed to be ignoring him. She tells him that she just wanted to feel that she could mingle and move about without having to be dependent on him. She explains that it wasn't anything personal and that she feels quite good about their relationship. Joe feels relieved and has a sense that he has come to a deeper understanding and appreciation of his wife. He also wonders whether or not he would have seen the oncoming car if he had resolved the issues with his wife before getting in the car. At this point, Joe feels relieved. He has some guilt for his part in the accident, even though the other person was clearly at fault for running the stop sign.

Tom then asks Joe to describe the details of the road just before he had the accident, even though Joe claims he doesn't remember what happened. As Joe begins to describe what he can recall, he feels both shoulders tighten and go up. He has a sensation of his body pulling away to the right, followed by the image of a flickering shadow. Tom asks his friend to look at the shadow, and as he does Joe begins to see the yellow color of a car (orienting response). As Joe tries to bring more detail to that image he realizes that he saw a front fender, and then the driver's face through the windshield of the car. Joe can tell from the look on his face that he is oblivious to the fact that he has just run a stop sign—the man seems to be lost in thought. Tom asks Joe what he is feeling and he says that he is really angry at the guy and wants to destroy him. Tom encourages Joe to imagine that he is destroying the other car. Joe sees himself getting a big hammer and smashing the other car to smithereens. He is now experiencing increased activation (more than he has before). His hands are trembling and shaking and have turned cold. Tom uses soothing words to support Joe through the process of releasing the energy. After some time, Joe begins to feel his breathing regulate, the tension in his shoulders and jaw relaxes, and the trembling settles. He has a sense of relief and warmth in his hands now. He feels relaxed and alert at the same time.

Joe now notices his shoulders pulling up and off to the right. He becomes aware of his arm wanting to turn the wheel to the right just as he hears the crash and buckling of metal. Tom asks Joe to ignore the crash for the moment, focus on the sensation, and complete the turn to the right. Joe makes the turn in his body and "avoids" the accident. He has some more mild shaking that is quickly followed by a tremendous amount of relief—even though he knows the accident did happen.

Tom asks Joe to return to the point where he first saw the yellow fender and the man through the windshield. From there they move to the moment where he hears the first clang of metal. As these images are accessed, Joe feels his body being thrown to the left, while at the same time, it is pulling back in the opposite direction. He feels like he is being propelled forward and his back muscles are trying, unsuccessfully, to pull him back. Tom encourages Joe to keep feeling his back muscles. Joe experiences increased tension as he focuses on the muscles. He then experiences a slight feeling of panic. At that point, Joe's back muscles release and he breaks into a sweat. He shakes and trembles deeply for several minutes. At the end of this, Joe discovers himself feeling peaceful and safe.

Joe knows that the accident happened. He knows that he tried to avoid it. He knows that he wanted to go back to talk to his wife. Each of these experiences are equally real for him. It doesn't seem like one is real and the others are made up; they appear as different outcomes to the same event, both equally real.

In the few days following the release of the energy stored in trauma, the symptoms in Joe's right arm and back cleared up significantly. It is important to recognize that the pain he was experiencing was related to impulses he had that had not been completed. The first impulse was to turn the steering wheel to the right and to go back to talk to his wife. The second was to turn right to avoid the accident. A third was the muscles in his back that were trying to pull him back. Being encouraged to *complete* each of these actions, Joe was able to release the stored energy associated with the impulses, even if it was after the fact.

We can see that this process offers a way to allow responses to complete and images to become more connected (associated). Images that are constricted become expanded, while stored energy is released through gradual discharge and completion—one step at a time.

17

First Aid for Children

Delayed Traumatic Reactions

Johnny, age five, proudly riding his first bicycle, hits loose gravel and careens into a tree. He is momentarily knocked unconscious. Getting up amid a flow of tears, he feels disoriented and somehow different. His parents hug him, console him, and put him back on the bike, all the while praising his courage. They do not realize how stunned and frightened he is.

Years after this apparently minor incident, John, driving with his wife and children, swerves to avoid an oncoming car. He freezes in the midst of the turn. Fortunately, the other driver is able to maneuver successfully and avoid catastrophe.

One morning several days later, John begins to feel restless while driving to work. His heart starts racing and pounding; his hands become cold and sweaty. Feeling threatened and trapped, he has a sudden impulse to jump out of the car and run. He acknowledges the "craziness" of his feelings, realizes no one was hurt, and gradually, the symptoms subside. A vague and nagging apprehension, however, persists most of the day. Returning home that evening without incident, he feels relieved.

The next morning, John leaves early to avoid the traffic and stays late to discuss business with some colleagues. When he arrives home, he is irritable and edgy. He argues with his wife and barks at the children. John goes to bed early. He is awakened in the middle of the night and faintly recalls a dream in which his car is sliding out of control. He is drenched in sweat. More fretful nights follow.

John is experiencing a delayed reaction sensitized by the bike accident he had as a child. Incredible as it may seem, post-traumatic reactions of this type are common. After working for more than twenty-five years with people suffering from trauma, I can say that at least half of my clients have had traumatic symptoms that remained dormant for a significant period of time before surfacing. For many people, the interval between the event and the onset of symptoms is between six weeks and eighteen months. However, the latency period can last for years or even decades. In both instances, the reactions are often triggered by seemingly insignificant events.

Of course, not every childhood accident produces a delayed traumatic reaction. Some have no residual effect at all. Others, including those viewed as "minor" and forgotten incidents of childhood, can have significant aftereffects. A fall, a seemingly benign surgical procedure, the loss of a parent through death or divorce, severe illness, even circumcision and other routine medical procedures can all cause traumatic reactions later in life, depending on how the child experiences them at the time they occur.

Of these traumatic antecedents, medical procedures are by far the most common and potentially the most impacting. Many clinics (unintentionally) amplify the fear of an already frightened child. In preparation for some routine procedures, infants are strapped into "papooses" to keep them from moving. A child that struggles so much that he or she needs to be tied down, however, is a child too frightened to be restrained without suffering the consequences. Likewise, a child who is severely frightened is not a good candidate for anesthesia until a sense of tranquillity has been restored. A child induced into anesthesia while frightened will almost certainly be traumatized—often severely. Children can even be traumatized by insensitively administered enemas or thermometers.

Much of the trauma associated with medical procedures can be prevented if health care providers do the following:

1. Encourage parents to stay with their children.
2. Explain as much as possible in advance.
3. Delay procedures until the children are calm.

The problem is that few professionals understand trauma or the lasting and pervasive effects these procedures can have. Although medical personnel are often quite concerned with the children's welfare, they may need more information from you, the consumer.

First Aid for Accidents and Falls

Accidents and falls are a normal and often benign part of growing up. However, occasionally a child may experience a traumatic reaction from one of these everyday occurrences. Witnessing a mishap of this sort will not necessarily clue you in to the degree of its severity. A child can be traumatized by events that seem relatively insignificant to an adult. It is important to be aware of the fact that children can be quite adept at covering up the signs of traumatic impact, especially when they feel that "not being hurt" will keep mommy and daddy happy. Your best ally in responding to your child's needs is an informed perspective.

Here are some guidelines:

Attend to your own responses first, inwardly acknowledging your concern and fear for the injured child. Take a deep breath and exhale slowly; sense the feelings in your own body. If you feel upset, do it again. The time it takes to establish a sense of calm is time well spent. It will increase your capacity to attend fully to the child, while minimizing the child's reaction to your own fear or confusion. If you have the time to gather yourself, your own acceptance of the accident will help you focus on the child's needs. If you are too emotional you carry the potential to frighten the child as much as the accident has. Children are very sensitive to the emotional states of all adults, but particularly their parents.

Keep the child quiet and still. If the injury requires immediate movement, support or carry the child, even if he/she appears capable of moving on his/her own. Children who make great efforts to show their strength often do so to deny the fear they are feeling. If you sense that the child is cold, gently drape a sweater or blanket over his/her shoulders and trunk.

Encourage (insist, if necessary) the child to take sufficient time to rest in a safe place. This is of particular importance if you notice signs of shock or dazedness (glazed eyes, pale complexion, rapid or shallow breathing, trembling, disorientation, a sense of being somewhere else). If the child's demeanor is excessively emotional or overly calm (before the storm), rest is very important. You can help the child settle down by being relaxed, quiet, and still yourself. If hugging or holding seem appropriate, do so in a gentle, non-restricting way. A gentle placement of your hand in the center of the back, behind the heart, can communicate support and reassurance without interfering with the child's natural bodily responses. Excessive patting or rocking can interrupt the recovery process (similar to the over-zealous child who, with good intentions, mishandles a wounded bird).

As the dazed look begins to wear off, carefully guide the child's attention to his/her sensations. In a soft voice, ask, "What do you feel in your body?" Slowly and quietly, repeat the answers you're given in the form of a question—"You feel bad in your body?"—then wait for a nod or other response. You can be more specific with your next question: "Where do you feel that bad feeling?" (let the child show you). If the child points to a specific place, ask, "How do you feel in your tummy (head, arm, leg, etc.)?" If the child reports a distinct sensation, gently inquire about its exact location, size, shape, color, weight, and other characteristics. Gently guide the child to the present moment (i.e., "How does the lump (owie, scrape, burn, etc.) feel now?"

Allow a moment or two of silence between questions. This will permit the completion of any cycle that the child is moving through without the distraction of another question. If you are uncertain whether the cycle has been completed, wait for the child to give you cues (a deep relaxed breath, the cessation of crying or trembling, a stretch, a smile, the making or breaking of eye contact). The completion of this cycle may not mean that the recovery process is over. Another cycle may follow. Keep the child focused on sensations for a few more minutes just to make sure the process is complete.

Do not stir up discussion about the accident. There will be plenty of time later for telling stories about it, playing it through, or drawing pictures of it. Now is the time for discharge and rest.

Validate the child's physical responses throughout this period of time. Children often begin to cry or tremble as they come out of shock. If you have a desire to stop this natural process, *resist it.* The physical expression of distress needs to continue until it stops or levels out on its own. The completion of this process usually takes a few minutes. Studies show that children who take this opportunity after an accident have fewer problems recovering.

Your task is to let the child know that crying and trembling are normal, healthy reactions. A reassuring hand on the back or shoulder, along with a few gently spoken words such as "That's OK," or "That's good—just let the scary stuff shake right out of you," can help immensely. Your primary function is to create a safe environment for the child to complete his/her natural responses to being hurt. Trust the child's innate ability to heal. Trust your own ability to allow this to happen. To avoid unintentional disruption of the process, don't shift the child's position, distract his/her attention, hold the child too tightly, or position yourself too close or too far away for comfort. Notice when the child begins to re-orient him/herself to the external world. Orientation is a sign of completion.

Finally, attend to the child's emotional responses. Once the youngster appears safe and calm (not before, but later is fine), set aside time for storytelling or for re-enacting the incident. Begin by asking the child to tell you what happened. He/she may be experiencing anger, fear, sadness, embarrassment, shame, or guilt. Tell the child about a time when you, or someone you know, felt the same way or had a similar accident. This will help "normalize" what the child is feeling. Let the youngster know that whatever he/she is feeling is OK and worthy of attention. While applying these first-aid measures, trust yourself. Don't think too much about whether you're "doing it right."

Trauma cannot always be prevented; it's a fact of life. But it can be healed. It is an interrupted process naturally inclined to complete itself whenever possible. If you create the opportunity, your child will complete this process and avoid the debilitating effects of trauma.

Resolving a Traumatic Reaction

Creating an opportunity for healing is similar to learning the customs of a new country. It is not difficult-just different. It requires you and your child to shift from the realm of thought or emotion to the much more basic realm of physical sensation. The primary task is to pay attention to how things feel and how the body is responding. In short, opportunity revolves around sensation.

A traumatized child who is in touch with internal sensations is paying attention to impulses from the reptilian core. As a result, the youngster is likely to notice subtle changes and responses, all of which are designed to help discharge excess energy and to complete feelings and responses that were previously blocked. Noticing these changes and responses enhances them.

The changes can be extremely subtle: something that feels internally like a rock, for example, may suddenly seem to melt into a warm liquid. These changes have their most beneficial effect when they are simply watched, and not interpreted. Attaching meaning to them or telling a story about them at this time may shift the child's perceptions into a more evolved portion of the brain, which can easily disrupt the direct connection established with the reptilian core.

Bodily responses that emerge along with sensations typically include involuntary trembling, shaking, and crying. The body may want, slowly, to move in a particular way. If suppressed or interrupted by beliefs about being strong (grown up, courageous), acting normal, or abiding by familiar feelings, these responses will not be able to effectively discharge the accumulated energy.

Another feature of the level of experience generated by the reptilian core is the importance of rhythm and timing. Think about it...everything in the wild is dictated by cycles. The seasons turn, the moon waxes and wanes, tides come in and go out, the sun rises and sets. Animals follow the rhythms of nature—mating, birthing, feeding, hunting, sleeping, and hibernating in direct response to nature's pendulum. So, too, do the responses that bring traumatic reactions to their natural resolution.

For human beings, these rhythms pose a two-fold challenge. First, they move at a much slower pace than we are accustomed to. Second, they are entirely beyond our control. Healing cycles can only be opened up to, watched, and validated; they cannot be evaluated, manipulated, hurried, or changed. When they get the time and attention they need, they are able to complete their healing mission.

Immersed in the realm of instinctual responses, your child will undergo at least one such cycle. How can you tell when it is complete? Tune in to your child. Traumatized children who remain in the sensing mode without engaging their thought processes feel a release and an opening; their attention then focuses back on the external world. You will be able to sense this shift in your child, and know that healing has taken place.

Resolving a traumatic reaction does much more than eliminate the likelihood of reactions emerging later in life. It fosters an ability to move through threatening situations with greater ease. It creates, in essence, a natural resilience to stress. A nervous system accustomed to moving into stress and then out of it is healthier than a nervous system burdened with an ongoing, if not accumulating, level of stress. Children who are encouraged to attend to their instinctual responses are rewarded with a lifelong legacy of health and vigor.

How Can I Tell If My Child Has Been Traumatized?

Any unusual behavior that begins shortly after a severely frightening episode or medical procedure, particularly with anesthesia, may indicate that your child is traumatized. Compulsive, repetitive mannerisms (such as repeatedly smashing a toy car into a doll) are an almost sure sign of an unresolved reaction to a traumatic event. (The activity may or may not be a literal replay of the trauma.) Other signs of traumatic stress include:

1. persistent, controlling behaviors
2. regression to earlier behavior patterns, such as thumb-sucking
3. tantrums, uncontrollable rage attacks
4. hyperactivity
5. a tendency to startle easily
6. recurring night terrors or nightmares, thrashing while asleep, bed-wetting
7. inability to concentrate in school, forgetfulness
8. excessive belligerence or shyness, withdrawal or fearfulness
9. extreme need to cling
10. stomachaches, headaches, or other ailments of unknown origin.

To find out whether an uncustomary behavior is indeed a traumatic reaction, try mentioning the frightening episode and see how your child responds. A traumatized child may not want to be reminded of the predisposing event, or conversely, once reminded, will become excited or fearful and unable to stop talking about it.

Reminders are revealing retrospectively as well. Children who have "outgrown" unusual behavior patterns have not necessarily discharged the energy that gave rise to them. The reason traumatic reactions can hide for years is that the maturing nervous system is able to control the excess energy. By reminding your child of a frightening incident that precipitated altered behaviors in years past, you may well stir up signs of traumatic residue.

Reactivating a traumatic symptom need not be cause for concern. The physiological processes involved, primitive as they are, respond well to interventions that both engage and allow them to follow the natural course of healing. Children are wonderfully receptive to experiencing the healing side of a traumatic reaction. Your job is simply to provide an opportunity for this to occur.

Sammy: A Case History

The following is an example of what can happen when a relatively common incident goes awry:

Sammy has been spending the weekend with his grandmother and step-grandfather, where I am their guest. Sammy is being an impossible tyrant, aggressively and relentlessly trying to control his new environment. Nothing pleases him; he is in a foul temper every waking moment. When he is asleep, he tosses and turns as if wrestling with his bedclothes. This is not behavior entirely unexpected from a two-and-a-half-year-old whose parents have gone away for the weekend—children with separation anxiety often act it out. Sammy, however, has always enjoyed visiting his grandparents and this behavior seems extreme to them.

His grandparents stated that six months earlier, Sammy fell off his high chair and split his chin open. Bleeding profusely, he was taken to the local emergency room. When the nurse came to take his temperature and blood pressure, he was so frightened that she was unable to record his vital signs. The two-year-old-child was subsequently strapped down in a "pediatric papoose" (a board with flaps and Velcro straps), with his torso and legs immobilized. The only part of his body he could move was his head and neck—which, naturally, he did, as energetically as he could. The doctors responded by tightening the restraint in order to suture his chin.

After this upsetting experience, Mom and Dad took Sammy out for a hamburger and then to the playground. His mother was very attentive and carefully validated his experience of being scared and hurt, and all seemed forgotten. However, the boy's tyrannical attitude began shortly after this event. Could Sammy's over-controlling behavior be related to his perceived helplessness from this trauma?

I discovered that Sammy had been to the emergency room several times with various injuries, though he had never exhibited this degree of terror and panic. When the parents returned, we agreed to explore whether there might be a traumatic charge still associated with this recent experience.

We all assembled in the cabin where I was staying. Sammy wouldn't have anything to do with talking about the fall or the hospital experience. With parents, grandparents, and Sammy watching, I precariously placed his stuffed Pooh Bear on a chair, where it fell off and had to be taken to the hospital. Sammy shrieked, bolted for the door, and ran across a foot bridge and down a narrow path to the creek. Our suspicions were confirmed. His most recent visit to the hospital was neither benign nor forgotten. Sammy's behavior indicated that this game was potentially overwhelming for him.

Sammy's parents brought him back from the creek. He clung frantically to his mother. As we readied for another game, we reassured him that we would all be there to help protect Pooh Bear. Again he ran—but this time he ran into my bedroom. We followed him into the bedroom and waited to see what would happen next. Sammy ran to the bed and hit it with both arms while looking at me expectantly. Interpreting this as a go-ahead sign, I put Pooh Bear under a blanket and placed Sammy on the bed next to him.

"Sammy, let's all help Pooh Bear."

I held Pooh Bear under the blanket and asked everyone to help. Sammy watched with interest, but soon got up and ran to his mother. Clinging to her he said, "Mommy, I'm scared." Without pressuring him, we waited until Sammy was ready and willing to play the game again. The next time Grandma and Pooh Bear were held down together and Sammy actively participated in their rescue. When Pooh Bear was freed, Sammy ran to his mother, clinging even more acutely in fear, but also with a growing sense of excitement, triumph, and pride, his chest open and held high. The next time he held on to mommy there was less clinging and more excited jumping. We waited until Sammy was ready to play again. Everyone except Sammy took a turn being rescued with Pooh. With each rescue, Sammy became more vigorous as he pulled off the blanket.

When it was Sammy's turn to be held under the

blanket with Pooh Bear, he became quite agitated and fearful and ran back to his mother's arms several times before he was able to accept the ultimate challenge. Bravely, he climbed under the blankets with Pooh while I held the blanket gently down. I watched his eyes grow wide with fear, but only momentarily. Then he grabbed Pooh Bear, shoved the blanket away, and flung himself into his mother's arms. Sobbing and trembling, he screamed, "Mommy, get me out of here. Mommy, get this thing off of me." His startled father told me that these were the same words Sammy screamed while imprisoned in the papoose at the hospital. He remembered this clearly because he had been quite surprised by his son's ability to make such a direct, articulate demand at two-plus years of age.

We went through the escape several more times. Each time, Sammy exhibited more power and more triumph. Instead of running fearfully to his mother, he jumped excitedly up and down. With every successful escape, we all clapped and danced together, cheering, "Yeah for Sammy, yeah, yeah, Sammy saved Pooh Bear." Two-and-a-half-year-old Sammy had mastered the experience that shattered him a few months ago.

What might have happened if we hadn't made this intervention? Would Sammy have become more anxious, hyperactive, and controlling? Might the trauma have resulted in restricted and less adaptive behaviors later? Might he have re-enacted the event decades later, or would he have developed inexplicable symptoms (e.g., tummy aches, migraines, anxiety attacks) without knowing why? Clearly, all of these scenarios are possible—and equally impossible to pin down. We cannot know how, when, or even whether a child's traumatic experience will invade his or her life in another form.

However, we can help protect our children from these possibilities through prevention. We can also help them develop into surer, more spontaneous adults.

Traumatic Play, Re-enactment, and Renegotiation

It is important to appreciate the difference between traumatic play, traumatic re-enactment, and the re-working of trauma as we saw with Sammy. Traumatized adults often re-enact an event that in some way represents, at least to their unconscious, the original trauma. Similarly, children re-create traumatic events in their play. While they may not be aware of the significance behind their behaviors, they are deeply driven by the feelings associated with the original trauma to re-enact them. Even if they won't talk about the trauma, traumatic play is one way a child will tell his or her story of the event.

In *Too Scared To Cry*[14], Lenore Terr describes the play and responses of three-and-a-half-year-old Lauren as she plays with toy cars. "The cars are going on the people," Lauren says as she zooms two racing cars toward some finger puppets. "They're pointing their pointy parts into the people. The people are scared. A pointy part will come on their tummies, and in their mouths, and on their… [she points to her skirt]. My tummy hurts. I don't want to play any more." Lauren stops herself as this bodily symptom of fear abruptly surfaces. This is a typical reaction. She may return over and over to the same play, and each time she will stop when fear arises in the form of her tummy hurting. Some psychologists would say that Lauren is using her play as an attempt to gain some control over the situation that traumatized her. Her play does resemble "exposure" treatments used routinely to help adults overcome phobias. Terr points out, however, that such play is quite slow in healing the child's dis-

---

[14] Basic Books, 1984

tress—if it ever does. Most often, the play is compulsively repeated without resolution. Unresolved, repetitious traumatic play can reinforce the traumatic impact in the same way that re-enactment and cathartic reliving of traumatic experiences can reinforce trauma in adults.

The re-working or *renegotiation* of a traumatic experience, as we saw with Sammy, represents a process that is fundamentally different from traumatic play or re-enactment. Left to their own devices, most children will attempt to avoid the traumatic feelings that their play invokes. With guidance, Sammy was able to "live his feelings through" by gradually and sequentially mastering his fear. Using this stepwise renegotiation of the traumatic event and Pooh Bear's support, Sammy was able to emerge as the victor and hero. A sense of triumph and heroism almost always signals the successful conclusion of a renegotiated traumatic event.

Key Principles for Renegotiating Trauma with Children

I will use Sammy's experience in discussing the following principles:

1. Let the child control the pace of the game. By running out of the room when Pooh Bear fell off the chair, Sammy told us quite clearly that he was not ready to play this new activating game. Sammy had to be "rescued" by his parents, comforted, and brought back to the scene before continuing. We all had to assure Sammy that we would be there to help protect Pooh Bear. By offering this support and reassurance, we helped Sammy move closer to playing the game.

When Sammy ran into the bedroom instead of out the door, he was telling us that he felt less threatened and more confident of our support. Children may not state verbally whether they want to continue; take cues from their behavior and responses. Respect their wishes, as well as the mode in which they choose to communicate. Children should never be forced to do more than they are willing and able to do. Slow down the process if you notice signs of fear, constricted breathing, stiffening, or a dazed (dissociated) demeanor. These reactions will dissipate if you simply wait quietly and patiently while reassuring the child that you are still there. Usually, the youngster's eyes and breathing will tell you when it's time to continue. Read Sammy's story again and pay particular attention to the places that indicate his decision to continue the game. There are three explicit examples in addition to the one cited above.

2. Distinguish between fear, terror, and excitement. Experiencing fear or terror for more than a brief moment during traumatic play will not help the child move through the trauma. Most children will take action to avoid it. Let them. At the same time, be certain that you can discern whether it is avoidance or escape. When Sammy ran down the creek, he was demonstrating avoidance behavior. In order to resolve his traumatic reaction, Sammy had to feel that he was in control of his actions rather than driven to act by his emotions. Avoidance behavior occurs when fear and terror threaten to overwhelm the child. This behavior is usually accompanied by some sign of emotional distress (crying, frightened eyes, screaming). Active escape, on the other hand, is exhilarating. Children will become excited by their small triumphs and often show pleasure by glowing with smiles, clapping their hands, or laughing heartily. Overall, the response is much different from avoidance behavior.

Excitement is evidence of the child's successful discharge of emotions that accompanied the original experience. This is positive, desirable, and necessary. Trauma is transformed by changing intolerable feelings and sensations into palatable ones. This can only happen at a level of activation that is similar to the activation that led to the traumatic reaction. If the child appears excited, it is OK to offer encouragement, and continue as we did when we clapped and danced with Sammy. If the child appears frightened or cowed, on the other hand, give reassurance but don't encourage any further movement at this time. Be present with your full attention, support, and reassurance; wait patiently while the fear subsides.

3. Take one small step at a time. You can never move too slowly in renegotiating a traumatic event. Traumatic play is repetitious almost by definition. Make use of this cyclical characteristic. The key difference between renegotiation and traumatic play is that in renegotiation there are small incremental differences in the child's responses and behaviors. When Sammy ran into the bedroom instead of out the door, he was responding with a different behavior—this is a sign of progress. No matter how many repetitions it takes, if the child is responding differently, even slightly—with more excitement, with more speech, with more spontaneous movements-the child is moving through the trauma. If the child's responses appear to be moving in the direction of constriction or repetition instead of expansion and variety, you may be attempting to renegotiate the event with scenarios that involve too much progress for your child to make at once. Slow down the rate of change and if that doesn't seem to help, re-read this chapter and look more closely at the role you are playing and how the child is responding; perhaps there are some signals you are missing.

We engaged Sammy in playing the game with Pooh Bear at least ten times. Sammy was able to renegotiate his traumatic responses fairly quickly. Another child might require more time. Don't be concerned about how many times you have to go through what seems to be the same old thing. If the child is responding, forget your concerns and enjoy the game.

4. Be patient—A Good Container. Remember that nature is on your side. For the adult, perhaps the most difficult and important aspect of renegotiating a traumatic event with a child is maintaining your own belief that things will turn out OK. This feeling comes from inside of you and is projected out to the child. It becomes a container that surrounds the child with a feeling of confidence. This may be particularly difficult if your child resists your attempts to renegotiate the trauma. Be patient and reassuring. A big part of the child wants to re-work this experience. All you have to do is wait for that part to assert itself. If you are excessively worried about whether the child's traumatic reaction can be transformed, you may inadvertently send a conflicting message to your child. Adults with their own unresolved trauma may be particularly susceptible to falling into this trap. Don't let your child suffer as a result of your own unresolved experiences. Ask someone else to help the child and help yourself.

5. If you feel that your child is genuinely not benefiting from the play, stop. Sammy was able to renegotiate his experience in one session, but not all children will. Some children may take a few sessions. If, after repeated attempts, the child remains constricted and does not move toward triumph and joy, do not force the issue. Consult qualified professional help.

Healing trauma in children is an immensely important and complex issue. Consequently, I am now working on a book dedicated solely to this subject. It will include detailed information that can be used by parents, teachers, and therapists.

"Curse the mind that mounts the clouds
in search of mythical kings and only mystical things,
mystical things
cry for the soul that will not face
the body as an equal place
and I never learned to touch for real
down, down, down where the iguanas feel."
—"Iguana Song" by Judy Mayham

Epilogue
Three Brains, One Mind

In our exploration of trauma we have learned about the primordial energies that reside within the reptilian core of our brains. We are not reptiles, but without clear access to our reptilian and mammalian heritage, we are not able to be fully human. The fullness of our humanity lies in the ability to integrate the functions of our triune brain.

We see that to resolve trauma we must learn to move fluidly between instinct, emotion, and rational thought. When these three sources are in harmony, communicating sensation, feeling, and cognition, our organisms operate as they were designed to.

In learning to identify and contact bodily sensations we begin to fathom our instinctual reptilian roots. In themselves, instincts are merely reactions. However, when these reactions are integrated and expanded by our mammalian feeling brain and our human cognitive abilities in an organized fashion, we experience the fullness of our evolutionary heritage.

It is important to understand that the more primitive portions of our brains are not exclusively survival-oriented (just as our modern brain is not exclusively cognitive). They carry vital information about who we are. The instincts not only tell us when to fight, run, or freeze, they tell us that we belong here. The sense that "I am I" is instinctual. Our mammalian brains broaden that sense to "We are we"—that we belong here together. Our human brains add a sense of reflection and connection beyond the material world.

Without a clear connection to our instincts and feelings, we cannot feel our connection and sense of belonging to this earth, to a family, or anything else.

Herein lie the roots of trauma. Disconnection from our felt sense of belonging leaves our emotions floundering in a vacuum of loneliness. It leaves our rational minds to create fantasies based on disconnection rather than connection. These fantasies compel us to compete, make war, distrust one another, and undermine our natural respect for life. If we do not sense our connection with all things, then it is easier to destroy or ignore these things. Human beings are naturally cooperative and loving. We enjoy working together. However, without fully integrated brains, we cannot know this about ourselves.

In the process of healing trauma we integrate our triune brains. The transformation that occurs when we do this fulfills our evolutionary destiny. We become completely human animals, capable of the totality of our natural abilities. We are fierce warriors, gentle nurturers, and everything in between.

Index

GERRY GREENBERG

Peter Levine received his Ph.D. in Medical and Biological Physics from the University of California at Berkeley. He also holds an independent doctorate degree in Psychology from International University. During his thirty year study of stress and trauma, he has contributed to a variety of scientific and medical publications, including the chapter on stress in *The Handbook of Psychophysiology.*

He was a consultant for NASA during the development of the Space Shuttle, and has taught at hospitals and pain clinics in both Europe and the US, as well as at the Hopi Guidance Center in Arizona. He is currently a consultant for the Pain-Rehabilitation Center in Boulder, Colorado.

Dr. Levine lives in the foothills of the Rockies, on the banks of the St. Vrain River, near Lyons, Colorado.

Further Information

For further information about books and other resources on Trauma, including childhood trauma, Professional Practitioners, public lectures or professional training programs, contact:

SOMATIC EXPERIENCING® TRAUMA INSTITUTE
a not-for-profit organization

6685 Gunpark Drive
Suite 201
Boulder, CO 80301
Phone: 303-652-4035
Fax: 303-652-4039

Email: info@traumahealing.org
Web Site: www.traumahealing.org